SHATTERED BUT STANDING

SHATTERED BUT STANDING

SHATTERED BUT STANDING

FROM BROKENESS TO BEAUTY THROUGH FAITH AND FORGIVENESS

Debra M Wright

RMKI PUBLISHING
PICKERING

Scripture quotations are taken from the **Holy Bible, New International Version® (NIV)** unless otherwise noted. Copyright © 1973, 1978, 1984, 2011 by Biblica, Inc. Used by permission. All rights reserved worldwide.

Published by *RMKI Press is a faith-inspired imprint of RMKI Publishing dedicated to producing books that encourage healing, forgiveness, and transformation. Our mission is to amplify voices that bring hope, empower purpose, and honour the power of story.*

Ontario Canada

ISBN: 978-1-0696156-3-3

Cover and Interior Design: Debra Wright &

Stonehouse Media

Printed in Canada

This book was produced with Pressbooks (https://pressbooks.com) and rendered with Prince.

Contents

Part I. Main Body

INTRODUCTION

We all walk through storms such as divorce, betrayal, loss, or disappointment. These moments threaten to shatter us. For a long time, I believed my brokenness would define me forever. But God had another plan. He took the very pieces of my pain and wove them into a testimony of forgiveness and freedom.

This book is not only my story. It is also a guide for your story. Each chapter will invite you to reflect, to release, and to rise. Through scriptures, affirmations, and practical tools, you will learn how to acknowledge your pain, release what holds you back, and empower yourself to step into the life God has designed for you.

My prayer is that as you read these pages, you will discover the courage to forgive, the strength to heal, and the joy of living a life that is truly free.

DEDICATION

To every woman who has ever felt shattered by life's storms, this book is for you. May you discover the beauty of forgiveness that mends the deepest wounds, the freedom of faith that lifts burdens you thought you would carry forever, and the joy of standing tall in your God-given purpose.

You are not defined by your brokenness, but by the strength and grace that rise from it. My prayer is that these words will remind you that your story is not over, and that even in the hardest chapters, God is still writing something beautiful.

And to my beloved children and precious grandchildren, you are my living reminders that hope always rises. Your love, your laughter, and your presence in my life continually show me that God's promises are faithful. This journey is richer because of you, and it's with all my heart that I dedicate this work to you.

ACKNOWLEDGE

This book is the result of countless prayers, tears, and moments of grace. It was born in the valleys of pain and refined on the mountaintops of God's mercy. I am deeply grateful to my family for standing beside me through seasons of brokenness and renewal. Your love, patience, and quiet strength gave me the courage to keep pressing forward when I wanted to give up.

A special thank you to my spiritual mentors and church family, Prophet Pearry, Pastor Vanya Caprietta, Prophetess Ruth Dente, and my mother, Dr. Maria Caprietta. Each of you carried me in prayer when I could not find the words myself. Your intercession, encouragement, and unwavering faith reminded me that I was never alone.

To the women I have coached, prayed with, and cried alongside, you are the heartbeat of these pages. Your courage and resilience inspired me to write honestly and to keep walking the road of forgiveness myself. Each story, including my own, is proof that God specializes in turning ashes into beauty.

Finally, I bow my heart in gratitude to my Heavenly Father. Without His love, forgiveness, and relentless pursuit of my soul, these words would not exist. Every chapter is a testimony of His faithfulness, and all glory belongs to Him.

FOREWORD

Releasing hurt, bitterness, anger, and disappointment is one of the hardest things a person will ever do, especially after betrayal and loss. For most people, trying to do it alone feels impossible.

I have watched Debra Wright walk through a devastating divorce and come out the other side not hardened, but refined. Kinder. Stronger. Clearer. That kind of transformation does not happen by accident.

Shattered but Standing is not a theory. It is a lived truth. Debra does not write as someone who avoids pain. She writes as someone who faced it head-on, processed it thoroughly, and learned how to release it through faith and forgiveness.

Healing can be accelerated when the right guide shows you the path. This book, and Debra's voice, can help you lay down what you were never meant to carry alone and begin again with strength, clarity, and peace.

Dr. Keith Johnson
America's #1 Confidence Coach®
Founder, 83K Academy

1.

WHEN FOREVER ENDS

For twenty-five years, I thought my marriage was safe. We had survived ups and downs, financial struggles, health challenges, and the many demands of raising children together. I believed that love and faith would hold us through anything. I grew up in a family where commitment and family prayer were sacred. My parents demonstrated that two people could endure storms together, and I carried that vision into my own marriage. I was convinced it would be forever.

I was only twenty-one years old when we got married. I was young and unprepared in many ways, yet determined to build a life together. In those early years, we faced obstacles that felt overwhelming. We did not yet have proper Canadian status, which made everything harder. My husband worked whenever he could find small jobs, and I did babysitting to help keep us afloat. It was a humble beginning, yet I believed that love would carry us through.

We longed for children, but those dreams did not come easily. I experienced painful losses that left me feeling broken and empty. I carried life within me, only to lose it far too soon. My daughter was born at five months of gestation, and the grief of that loss left us devastated. A few months later, I became pregnant again, but tragedy struck once more. I lost my son, and in the process, I nearly lost my own life. Those were some of the darkest days I can remember. My body ached with loss, and my spirit was weary.

In 1990, I discovered I was pregnant again. That season, we were filled with both fear and fragile hope. Each day, I prayed that God would protect this child. My prayers were answered when my beautiful daughter was born in the winter of 1991. Holding her for the first time reminded me that God can bring life out of loss. Over the next two years, I gave birth to two sons, and for a time, our home was filled with laughter, energy, and the ordinary chaos of raising children.

I loved my husband, and I know he loved me too, but marriage was never simple. We were not only raising children and managing finances; we were also trying to reconcile differences in how we practiced our faith. Religion played a significant role in our relationship, sometimes as a source of strength and other times as a source of division. We made beautiful memories together. We went on road trips, attended baseball games at the Skydome in Toronto, and bought two homes. The last home was particularly special because we watched it being built from the ground up. It felt like a symbol of all we had worked for. Yet beneath those milestones, cracks were forming that we did not know how to repair.

The day we sold that house was the day our family came apart. For me, it symbolized not just the loss of property, but also the loss of stability, of dreams, and of the belief that our union was unbreakable. My children were devastated and angry. Having to start over was excruciating. My heart clung to the scripture, ***"Weeping may endure for a night, but joy comes in the morning."*** **(Psalm 30:5).** I repeated it to myself as if those words alone could hold me together.

Forever turned out to be shorter than I expected.

The day it ended felt unreal, as though I had stumbled into a nightmare from which I could not wake. Divorce was something that happened to other people, not me, not us. I could still hear the echoes of promises made at the altar, words I thought we both intended to keep. Yet there I was, standing in the ruins of what I had built my life around, wondering how everything had crumbled so quickly.

The Weight of Grief

The pain was sharp, rising and falling in unpredictable waves. Some mornings, I woke up numb, unable to feel anything at all. Other mornings, I woke up angry, ready to shout at the unfairness of it all. Tears came without warning, in the grocery store, while brushing my teeth, travelling on the train on my way to school, or in the middle of a simple conversation. At night, I stared at the ceiling and whispered questions into the dark. Was it my fault? Could I have done more? Why did love leave me after all these years? Why was I not enough?

And then came the silence. After twenty-five years of being "we," I was now just "me." The quiet in the house was deafening. I missed even the simple disagreements or the famous one, his silence, because at least they meant there was still a connection, still something alive between us.

My children were young adults by then, but divorce does not ask how old your children are before it breaks their hearts. They tried to be strong for me, and I tried to be strong for them. Still, I could see the questions in their eyes, the sadness they carried, and it hurt more to watch them struggle than to face my own grief.

The Strange Nature of Grief

Grief is sneaky. It is not tidy or predictable. It arrives in waves, disguised as anger one day, guilt the next, and sometimes even laughter at the most unexpected moments.

I remember one evening when I was crying so hard that I forgot the stove was on and burned dinner completely. My son walked into the kitchen, wrinkled his nose, and said with a smirk, "Well, Mom, at least you're smoking hot." We both burst out laughing, and that laughter cut through the heaviness like light breaking into a dark room. It reminded me that life was still happening, and I was still capable of joy, even if only for a fleeting moment.

Moments like that showed me that grief does not mean the end of laughter. It does not mean life has stopped. Grief is layered. You can cry one moment and smile the next. Both are signs that your heart is still alive.

Losing More Than a Marriage

Looking back, I realize this chapter of my life was not only about losing a marriage. It was about losing the identity I had wrapped so tightly around being a wife, a partner, and the glue that held my family together. The removal of that role left me feeling exposed, uncertain, and deeply vulnerable. For so many years, I had introduced myself through the lens of "us," not "me." My worth, my plans, even my dreams were tied to the life I had built with someone else. When that bond broke, it felt as though the very foundation of who I was crumbled with it.

Who was I without the title of Mrs.? Could I rebuild my life without the one person I thought would always be by my side? Those questions haunted me in the quiet moments when the house was still, and the only sound was the echo of my own thoughts. I often tell women that the end of a marriage is like a death in the family. Even when things were rough, even when there were arguments and disappointments, when it is finally over, the grief arrives like an unexpected guest. You mourn what was, what could have been, and even the parts that never truly existed.

The grief does not just come from losing a person. It comes from losing the rhythm of your days, the familiar voice in the house, the shared dreams that once shaped your tomorrows. It is the small things that cut the deepest—the empty chair at dinner, the missing ring on your finger, the silence where laughter used to live. You begin to question everything. Was it my fault? Could I have prayed harder, tried longer, loved better? The "what ifs" play on repeat, each one chipping away at your peace until you learn to surrender them to God.

There were moments when I felt invisible, as if the woman I had been no longer existed and the woman I was becoming had not yet appeared. That in-between space was painful. It was like walking through fog, trying to find my way without a map. I remember journaling one night, pouring out all my anger, confusion, and sorrow onto the page. I told God, "I don't even know who I am anymore." And in the stillness, I sensed a whisper in my spirit: *"You are Mine. You always have been."*

That whisper became my lifeline. It was the thread of hope I clung to when everything else felt like it had fallen apart. I did not have all the answers then, but I began to understand that my story was not finished. What I thought was the end was really the beginning of a new chapter, a chapter where I would learn to see myself not through the eyes of another, but through the eyes of God.

It was in that season of profound loss that I discovered something powerful: God never allows subtraction without the promise of restoration. He may remove something that you thought you could not live without, only to replace it with something far greater: Himself. In those quiet, broken moments, I realized He was not just mending the pieces of my heart. He was reshaping them.

Psalm 34:18 says, "The Lord is near to the brokenhearted and rescues those whose spirits are crushed." Each day I would repeat it, sometimes through tears, sometimes through clenched faith. The Lord was near. Even in my brokenness, I was not abandoned.

Over time, I began to rebuild, not the same way as before, but stronger, with a clearer vision and deeper faith. I learned that identity rooted in people can be shaken, but identity rooted in God stands firm. The woman who once felt lost without her title began to rise, not as "Mrs.," not as "ex-wife," but as Debra-a woman chosen, loved, and whole in Christ.

If you find yourself in that same place today, wondering who you are after loss, hear this truth: You are more than what you have lost. You are more than the titles or roles that once defined you. You are still loved, still seen, and still called for purpose. The story is not over. God is still writing.

God's Nearness in the Ruins

It was a promise that even in my brokenness, God was not far away. He was close, holding me, strengthening me, reminding me that even though my marriage had ended, my life had not.

There were days when I felt utterly abandoned, but His nearness showed up in unexpected ways. A friend is calling to check on me. A sermon that felt written just for my heart. A sunrise that reminded me that new mercies arrive every morning. God never left me in the ruins.

Reclaiming Identity

When everything familiar falls apart, you are left standing face-to-face with yourself. There are no titles to hide behind, no routines to fill the silence, and no roles to perform. It is just you and God. That was where my healing began.

In the early days, I struggled to recognize the woman in the mirror. She looked like me, but her eyes told a story of exhaustion, sorrow, and survival. I realized I had spent years pouring into everyone else and leaving little room for myself. I had loved deeply, served faithfully, and given my all, but now I was empty. I did not know what joy looked like outside of being someone's wife, mother, or caregiver. It was as if I had been written out of my own story.

So, I began asking a life-changing, straightforward question: *Who am I now?*

That question became my compass. It led me to rediscover passions I had long neglected. I started journaling again, not just about pain but about possibility. I wrote down dreams, visions, and prayers that had once seemed too far away. I began to walk, not just for exercise, but to breathe, to pray, and to listen. I found God's presence in the rustle of leaves, in the quiet rhythm of my steps, and in the stillness of early morning light. Each walk became a conversation with Him, and through those talks, I began to hear His voice, reminding me that God had not forgotten me.

Psalm 139:14 reminded me that I was "fearfully and wonderfully made." Those words became more than a verse. They became an affirmation. I began to declare them over myself daily. I reminded my heart that I was created on purpose, for purpose, and that no failed relationship could erase that truth. Slowly, I started to see glimpses of the woman God designed me to be: strong, creative, compassionate, and full of grace.

I also learned that reclaiming identity requires forgiveness. Not just forgiving others, but forgiving yourself for the things you did not know, for the times you stayed too long, or for the moments you thought you were not enough. True healing begins when you stop punishing yourself for the past and start embracing who you are becoming.

It was not an overnight process. Some days, I felt powerful and free. Other days, the weight of memory tried to pull me backward. But even then, I chose to keep moving forward, one prayer, one breath, one act of courage at a time.

I discovered that identity is not found in people, possessions, or positions. It is found in purpose. God reminded me that my worth was not tied to what was lost, but to what He placed inside of me. There was still a calling on my life. There were still stories to tell, women to encourage, and dreams to pursue. The same God who saw me in my brokenness was now calling me to rise.

One evening, while sitting by the water, I asked God to show me who I was through His eyes. I closed my eyes and let the sound of the waves still my thoughts. In that moment, I felt peace settle over me. It was as if He whispered, "You are My daughter. You are loved. You are chosen." Tears flowed freely, not from pain this time, but from relief. I realized I no longer needed anyone else to define my worth. My identity was safe in Him.

Isaiah 61:3 says that God gives us "a crown of beauty for ashes, the oil of joy for mourning, and a garment of praise for the spirit of heaviness." That promise became my truth. I began to exchange shame for grace, sorrow for joy, and fear for faith. I started dressing differently, smiling more often, and walking with renewed confidence. Not because everything in my life was perfect, but because my heart was healing.

Reclaiming my identity also meant rediscovering my voice. For too long, I had silenced my dreams out of fear of judgment or rejection. But now, I spoke boldly about forgiveness, faith, and resilience. I began to share my story not from a place of pain, but from a place of purpose. Every time I spoke, wrote, or encouraged another woman, I felt pieces of myself return. What once felt like loss was now becoming legacy.

I learned that God does not waste anything. Even the broken chapters serve a purpose when placed in His hands. He uses them to shape compassion, deepen wisdom, and prepare you for the next season. I was no longer the same woman I had been before my storm. I was wiser, more grounded, and more dependent on God's grace than ever before.

To the woman reading this who feels lost after loss, hear this truth: You are not defined by what you have been through. You are defined by who you are becoming in Christ. You are not broken beyond repair. You are being rebuilt, redefined, and restored for a greater purpose.

Each day you choose to rise, you reclaim a piece of your power. Each prayer you whisper is a declaration that your story is not over. Each act of self-love is an offering of gratitude to the God who made you whole.

The woman who once felt invisible now stands tall, not because life is perfect, but because she finally knows who she is. She is a woman of grace, resilience, and purpose. She is not who she was—and she never will be again.

A.R.E. Focus: Acknowledge the Shock and Pain of Loss

- **Acknowledge:** Be honest about the shock and the depth of the pain. Pretending you are fine does not help you heal. Naming your emotions is the first step toward releasing them into God's hands.

Reflection and Prayer
Reflection Questions

Take a few quiet moments to reflect on these questions in your journal or during your prayer time. Allow the Holy Spirit to speak to your heart.

1. In what ways have I tied my identity to roles, relationships, or titles that no longer define me?

2. What parts of myself have I neglected while caring for others?

3. How can I begin to see myself the way God sees me?

4. What dream or gift has God placed inside me that is ready to be revived?

5. What truth from God's Word can I speak over myself each morning to strengthen my identity in Him?

As you write your reflections, remember that this process is not about perfection. It is about awareness. Each honest answer opens the door to deeper healing and alignment with who God created you to be.

Daily Affirmations

Speak these words aloud until they take root in your spirit:

- God loves me, and my value does not depend on anyone's approval.

- I am no longer bound by who I used to be. I am renewed each day.

- My identity is found in Christ, not in my past or my pain.

- I am becoming stronger, wiser, and more confident in God's plan for my life.

- I choose to walk in purpose, peace, and joy today.

Prayer

Heavenly Father,

Thank you for reminding me that my identity was not lost in the storms of life. You have called me by name, and I belong to You. When I forget who I am, whisper Your truth to my heart. When I feel unseen, remind me that You see me and love me completely.

Please help me let go of the need to define myself through others' eyes. Teach me to see myself through Your Word and to embrace the woman You created me to be. Restore every part of my soul that has been weighed down by disappointment, shame, or fear.

I declare that I am free, forgiven, and full of purpose. I choose to walk in confidence, grace, and love as I step into this new season of becoming. Thank You, Lord, for making all things new in me.

In Jesus' name,
Amen.

Closing Thought

The end of my marriage was not the end of my story. It was the breaking point that led me to discover who I truly was apart from a title or a role. It was where I learned that God's love is not shaken by divorce papers, broken promises, or nights filled with tears. His presence remained. And from those ruins, He began to build something new.

Excerpt from **Becoming Debra Wright**. *Used with permission. All rights reserved.*

2.

IN THE EYE OF THE STORM

The days after my divorce felt like walking through a hurricane with no shelter in sight. I was angry one minute, sobbing the next, and then suddenly convinced I could power through on my own. It was chaos inside my heart and mind, and no one could see the full storm raging within me. Outwardly, I smiled when I had to. I went to work, answered calls, and told everyone I was "fine." Inwardly, I was drowning in a sea of confusion and pain.

Anger became my closest companion. It showed up in unexpected moments. I found myself snapping at the most minor things or crying over something as simple as a commercial on television. I replayed scenes from my marriage in a loop, like a movie I could not turn off. The arguments that never found resolution, the silent moments where I felt unseen, the promises that were broken, and the words spoken that still pierced my heart like shards of glass, I lived them over and over again.

Each memory felt like a wave crashing over me, pulling me deeper into regret. I tried to distract myself with busyness, but the ache followed me everywhere. I carried it into every room, every conversation, every prayer. My body carried the evidence of this inner war. My chest was tight, my stomach twisted into knots, and my jaw ached from clenching my teeth in restless sleep. Resentment was like acid, burning slowly and poisoning everything I touched.

Yet beneath the layers of anger, there was something even more painful: a quiet, persistent whisper of self-blame. I asked myself over and over, "What did I do wrong? Was I not enough? Could I have prayed harder, loved deeper, forgiven sooner?" The questions became a loop that played in my mind both day and night. It did not matter how many people told me it was not my fault. I still carried the weight of guilt like a cloak I could not remove.

That was the most challenging part of the storm. The battle was not just around me. It was inside me. I was fighting to forgive, to understand, and to let go all at once. There were moments I thought I was making progress, only to have one memory drag me back into the waves. I found myself wrestling not only with my disappointment in him but also with my own.

I had been raised to believe in commitment, in perseverance, and in the power of prayer to sustain a marriage. I truly believed that if I prayed enough and loved enough, everything could be fixed. When it ended, I felt like I had failed both God and myself. I remember sitting in church one Sunday, trying to sing along with the worship team, but my voice broke. I whispered to God, "Why didn't You stop this? Why didn't you heal it?" And in that moment, I felt nothing but silence. It felt as though heaven itself had closed its doors to me.

But what I did not realize then was that God had not abandoned me. He was not silent because He was absent. He was quiet because He was working. I needed to be still long enough to feel His presence again. The storm was not meant to destroy me. It was meant to reveal what was still unhealed within me.

As the days went by, I began to notice small flickers of grace. A friend showed up with dinner and refused to leave until I laughed. A random stranger complimented me on my smile when I least felt like smiling. My children's voices on the phone became a comfort, reminding me that I was still needed, still loved, and still part of something bigger than my pain.

Those moments did not erase the storm, but they reminded me that even in the darkest seasons, God sends glimpses of light. He places minor signs of His love around us, even when we are too broken to see clearly.

One evening, I sat on the edge of my bed and whispered through tears, "Lord, I cannot carry this anymore." That was the first honest prayer I had prayed in months. There was no polished language, no long list of words, surrender. And in that moment, something shifted. The storm did not end overnight, but the winds began to soften.

In Isaiah 43:2, God says, "When you pass through the waters, I will be with you; and when you pass through the rivers, they will not sweep over you." It did not promise that the storm would disappear, but it promised that I would not drown. The waves might rise, but His hand would hold me above them.

I realized that my healing would begin only when I stopped fighting the storm and started inviting God into it. I needed to stop asking "why" and start asking "what now?" What did He want to teach me in this season? What was He trying to restore within me?

The storm revealed what had been buried for years: unmet needs, ignored boundaries, and a pattern of self-sacrifice that had left me drained. It forced me to face the truth that I had often confused love with endurance and forgiveness with silence. I had allowed my identity to be swallowed by the roles I played, forgetting that I was more than someone's wife or caretaker. I was God's daughter.

There is something sacred about surviving a storm

that was meant to break you. You come out of it different, softer in some ways, stronger in others. I began to understand that anger and self-blame were not my enemies; they were signals pointing to deeper wounds that needed healing. Once I faced them honestly and in prayer, they began to lose their hold on me.

Over time, my conversations with God became less about the past and more about the future. I began to thank Him for protecting me from things I did not understand. I thanked Him for giving me the courage to stand, even when I wanted to give up. I learned that healing does not erase pain: it transforms it.

When you allow God into the storm, He does not always calm the waves right away. Sometimes, He calms you first. He teaches you to breathe again, to trust again, and to believe that the same wind that once tore everything apart can now carry you into something new.

So if you find yourself in the middle of your own storm today, know this: you are not alone. The winds may be fierce, the rain may blind you, but God is still in control. The same voice that spoke "Peace, be still" over the waters will speak that same peace over your heart.

The storm within you will not last forever. The waves will recede. The skies will clear. And when they do, you will see that even in your most broken moments, you were never truly alone. God was there, steady and faithful, holding you until the calm returned.

The Layers of the Storm

I did not realize at the time that anger and self-blame often go hand in hand. Anger points outward at others, while self-blame points inward at ourselves. Both can keep us trapped. Both can keep us circling the same emotional hurricane, never finding our way out. I wanted to escape, but I did not know how to stop replaying the past.

Grief has a way of becoming a storm with many layers. First comes the shock, like a sudden downpour. Then comes denial, the quiet voice that says, "This cannot be real." Anger crashes in like thunder, followed by guilt that rolls in like heavy clouds. Some days brought sadness so thick it felt like fog, obscuring any glimpse of hope. On rare days, light would break through, but the storm seemed determined to return.

God's Lighthouses

Yet even in the middle of that chaos, there were moments of light. God, in His mercy, sent lighthouses into my storm. They were not grand gestures or miraculous rescues. They were quiet, consistent beams of hope that kept me from losing myself completely.

A friend showed up at my door one evening with soup and stories that made me laugh until my stomach hurt. For a few precious moments, I forgot about the ache in my chest. A late-night phone call from one of my children, to say, "Mom, I love you," became a lifeline of comfort, reminding me I still had a reason to keep going. My church family surrounded me in prayer when I had no words left. They carried me when I could not carry myself.

Those small acts of love were not coincidences. They were divine appointments. God knew exactly what I needed, even when I did not have the strength to ask for it. Each prayer, each hug, and each unexpected kindness became a lighthouse; steady, reliable, and full of grace, guiding me back to shore when I felt lost at sea.

Teachable Moment: The Hidden Gift of Storms

Storms reveal what is fragile, but they also reveal what is strong. When everything familiar disappears, the shaking exposes what has always been unshakable.

During that season, I learned that God sometimes allows storms not to destroy us, but to reveal the depth of our roots. When the storm of divorce stripped away the identity I thought defined me, I discovered that I was still standing, not because of my own power, but because God had planted roots of faith deep within me.

I began to see that my faith was not built on circumstances, but on the character of God Himself. The winds could rage, the rain could fall, but the foundation of His love remained unmovable. I also discovered the loyalty of real friends who stood by me when others walked away. Their presence reminded me that love does not disappear when life changes.

Sometimes, the gift of a storm is clarity. It clears away what was false, leaving only what is real. I learned who I was without titles, without approval, and without validation. I learned that I could survive what I thought would destroy me.

The hidden gift of storms is this: they push you to discover the God who calms the waves inside you, even when the storm outside still rages.

The Silence After the Storm

Eventually, the loudest part of the storm gave way to silence. After years of being "we," I was now simply "me." The quiet in the house was deafening. I missed the noise, even the arguments, because at least they meant there was still something alive between us.

Loneliness became its own kind of storm. It was not as loud, but it was just as powerful. I had to learn how to sit with myself in the quiet, without reaching for distractions. I had to learn how to eat dinner at an empty table without feeling like something was missing. I had to face the echo of my own thoughts and trust that I could rebuild a life on my own.

In that silence, God began to speak to me again, not through thunder or lightning, but through whispers of peace. He reminded me that I was still His daughter, still loved, and still called for a purpose greater than my pain.

The silence became a classroom. I learned how to listen to my heart again. I learned how to pray, not just for survival, but for transformation. I began to see that stillness is not the absence of God's presence, but the space where He does His deepest work.

A.R.E. Focus: Acknowledge

The first step toward healing was not to escape the storm, but to **acknowledge** it. Pretending the storm was not real did not make it go away. Denying the pain only made it stronger. Naming my emotions was the first step toward taking their power away.

It is not a weakness to say, "I feel angry," or "I feel lost." It is a strength. It is courage to face what hurts and still believe that healing is possible. Acknowledgment opens the door to God's restoration.

Acknowledge: The storm of emotions without shame.

Release: The illusion of control and the lies of self-blame.

Empower: The belief that storms may shake you, but they cannot destroy you when God is your anchor.

Practical Tool: Anchor Mapping

When sailors face storms at sea, they drop anchor to hold steady. In the same way, we need anchors for our souls: truths, people, and practices that keep us grounded when life feels unstable.

Exercise: Anchor Mapping

Take a few quiet moments to reflect on your anchors. Write them down in your journal or post them where you can see them daily.

Identify three anchors that keep you steady. These can be:

- Scriptures that remind you of God's faithfulness, such as Isaiah 43:2.

- People who encourage you, speak life into you, and remind you of who you are.

- Practices that calm your spirit, such as journaling, prayer, worship, or walking in nature.

Every time you feel the storm rise within, return to your anchors. They will remind you that even when the waves crash, you are held secure by God's love.

Reflection Exercise

Take time to write down the storms you are currently

navigating. These may be emotional, relational, or spiritual.

1. What are the three storms you are facing right now?

2. For each one, list the anchors that are already in place.

3. Ask yourself, "What is one small step I can take this week to calm the storm inside me?"

Remember, healing is not about fixing everything at once. It is about choosing peace one moment at a time.

Daily Affirmation

"I am not defined by the storm I am in. God is with me, guiding me, and I will not be swept away."

Speak this affirmation over yourself every morning until it becomes truth in your heart.

A Story of Renewal

One Sunday after church, a woman approached me and shared her own storm. Her eyes glistened with tears as she said, "I went through a painful divorce years ago. I never thought I would survive, but I did. Storms make you stronger, not weaker. Every time the wind blew against me, it taught me to lean harder on God."

Her words became a second anchor in my journey. I carried them with me in the months that followed. They reminded me that storms are temporary. They do not last forever. They come to test the structure of your faith, not to destroy it.

Eventually, the skies clear. The waves settle. What remains is the strength that God built in you through the trial. You emerge not only standing, but standing stronger, wiser, and more deeply rooted in grace.

Closing Prayer

Heavenly Father,
Thank You for being my anchor in every storm. When the waves rise, and fear surrounds me, remind me that You are near. Help me to acknowledge my pain without shame and to trust that Your presence is greater than my fear.

Teach me to see the hidden gifts in my storm, the resilience, the faith, and the compassion that only You can build within me. Thank You for the lighthouses You have placed along my path, the people and promises that guide me back to peace.

Even when I feel lost, help me remember that I am never beyond Your reach. You are my refuge, my strength, and my peace. I rest in the assurance that the storm will pass, and when it does, I will still be standing by Your grace.

In Jesus' name,
Amen.

The storm may rage, but it will not last forever. Clouds eventually break. Waves eventually calm. And when they do, you will see that you have not only survived the storm: you have grown stronger because of it.

3.

THE DAWN OF RENEWAL

There comes a point when the tears dry just enough for you to realize that you cannot live in the storm forever. The grief is still there, but you start to feel a faint stirring inside, a whisper that says, "Maybe *I can heal*. It is soft at first, almost hesitant, as if afraid to hope again. Yet that whisper keeps coming, reminding you that pain is not the only thing that lives inside you. Somewhere deep within the cracks of your heart, life is still waiting to bloom.

Healing begins quietly. It does not announce itself with trumpets or grand signs. It often starts with the slightest flicker of courage, the moment you decide to stand when it would be easier to stay down. You may still be fragile, still uncertain, but a part of you begins to believe that there could be life after heartbreak. That belief, as small as it is, becomes the seed of transformation.

For me, it started with tiny steps. I wish I could tell you that I woke up one morning and felt strong, whole, and ready to conquer the world. I wish I could say I was instantly restored, ready to move forward with clarity and confidence. But the truth is that healing did not come wrapped in a lightning bolt moment. It came quietly, slowly, one fragile decision at a time.

Some mornings, the victory was getting out of bed and facing the day. Other days, it was choosing to eat something nourishing instead of numbing myself with distraction. There were moments when all I could do was whisper a prayer through tears, "God, please help me make it through today." Those prayers were not eloquent, but they were real. I believe God hears the most broken prayers because they come straight from the heart.

Healing looked like allowing myself to cry when the memories surfaced instead of pretending I was fine. It looked like writing down my thoughts in a journal and seeing, sometimes with surprise, how far I had already come. It looked like sitting in silence, letting the peace of God settle where chaos once ruled.

There were days when I took two steps forward and one step back. But even that was progress. Healing is not a straight road. It is a winding path with pauses, detours, and lessons along the way. The important thing is not how fast you move, but that you keep moving.

Every small act of courage, every decision to believe that tomorrow could be better, became a building block in my recovery. In those moments, I realized that God was not waiting for me to have it all together before He could begin His work in me. He was already there, walking with me in the slow, messy middle.

Little by little, the heaviness began to lift. I started to notice beauty again: the sound of laughter, the glow of sunlight through my window, the comfort of familiar worship songs. These were reminders that joy was still possible, that the storm had not stolen everything.

Looking back, I understand that God was teaching me patience and dependence on Him. Healing was not about erasing the pain but learning how to live beyond it. Each small step was sacred because it was a declaration of faith: faith that I would not stay broken forever, faith that God was making something new even when I could not see it.

It was in the stillness, not the speed, that I began to heal. And in that stillness, I found God's voice again:

gentle, reassuring, and steady. He was never rushing me. He invited me to keep taking the next step, trusting that He would lead me to peace.

The First Steps

I began by making myself get out of bed, even when I wanted to pull the sheets over my head and disappear. Every morning was a battle between the weight of sorrow and the whisper of hope. The bed felt safe, but it also held me captive. I knew that if I stayed there, I would sink deeper into despair. So, one morning, I took a deep breath, swung my legs over the edge, and stood up. It felt like a small act, but in that moment, it was a victory.

I forced myself to eat something more than coffee and crackers. For days, food had no taste, and I had no appetite for anything, not even the things I once loved. But one afternoon, I made a simple bowl of soup, sat at the table, and thanked God for the strength to nourish myself. That meal became a turning point. It was not about the food itself; it was about choosing to care for the body that God had given me, even when I did not feel like it.

I took walks, even when my legs felt like lead, and my heart felt too heavy to carry. The first few times, I walked with tears streaming down my face, hiding behind sunglasses so no one would see. I did not have a destination. I walked to remind myself that the world was still moving, that life was still happening around me, and that somehow, I was still part of it. I would feel the cool air against my skin, hear the crunch of leaves beneath my feet, and notice the way the light filtered through the trees. Little by little, I began to see beauty again.

Some days, I would walk just to the corner and turn back. Other days, I made it farther, letting the rhythm of my steps calm my thoughts. The world outside became my therapy room, and the simple act of walking became a prayer in motion. I did not always have the words to speak, but I knew that every step was a silent cry that said, "Lord, I am still here."

And then, one day, something unexpected happened. I laughed. It was not planned or forced. I was watching an old sitcom rerun, and something so ridiculous happened on the screen that I burst into laughter. It startled me at first. It had been so long since I heard that sound come from my own mouth. That laughter did not erase the pain, but it reminded me that joy still lived somewhere inside me.

I began to find humour in small moments like the day I tried to cook for one and nearly set off the smoke alarm again. I remember standing there with the burnt pan in my hand, shaking my head and smiling. It was messy, but it was real. Life was messy, too, but I was learning to live it again.

Those were not dramatic steps. They were simple, ordinary choices. Yet in those baby steps, I saw something powerful. God was not asking me to sprint into healing. He was not demanding perfection or instant transformation. He was asking me to trust Him with the next step. Just one. And then another.

Each step became an act of faith. Each small decision to keep moving became a prayer of surrender. God met me in those quiet, ordinary moments. He did not rush me. He did not scold me for being slow. Instead, He walked beside me, whispering, "Daughter, I am with you. Keep going."

Looking back now, I realize that healing rarely happens in grand gestures. It begins in the slow, steady rhythm of choosing life over despair, one decision at a time. Getting out of bed and eating an authentic meal, taking a walk and laughing again. These are the steps that rebuild a soul.

If you are in that place today, wondering if your small

efforts matter, let me tell you they do. Every time you choose to rise instead of retreat, you are declaring that the storm will not have the final say. Every small step is a seed planted in faith, and in time, those seeds will grow into strength, joy, and peace.

Because healing is not about running ahead, it is about learning to walk again slowly, faithfully, one step at a time, with God lighting the path before you.

Healing Is Not Linear

Some days I felt like I was making progress, only to wake up the next morning and feel like I was back at square one. Healing is not a straight line. It is more like a winding path with detours, pauses, and even circles. But each step matters.

There were mornings I woke with a new sense of strength, ready to face the day with hope. And there were mornings when grief came crashing back like a wave, leaving me gasping for air. Sometimes I could pray with confidence, and other times I could only whisper, "Lord, please help me." At first, I thought this meant I was failing. I believed that if I truly trusted God, I would no longer feel the sting of sadness. But I slowly began to understand that healing has its own rhythm. It is not a steady climb upward. It is a journey with valleys and mountaintops, with pauses and breakthroughs, with tears and laughter woven together.

Jeremiah 30:17 became my anchor: "But I will restore you to health and heal your wounds, declares the Lord." I clung to that verse as if my life depended on it. My heart felt like shattered glass, but God promised restoration. Not partial healing. Not patched-up brokenness. Full restoration.

That scripture reminded me that healing was not something I had to manufacture on my own. Restoration was God's work in me. My role was to show up, take the next step, and keep my heart open to His touch. There was peace in knowing that I did not have to fix myself. God was already at work behind the scenes, even in the moments that felt still and silent.

Over time, I began to see that the days that felt like setbacks were not wasted. They were part of the process. On the hard days, I learned how to lean on God more deeply. I learned to be gentle with myself, to rest when I needed to, and to remember that healing is not measured by perfection, but by progress.

There were nights when I cried until I had no tears left, only to wake the next morning with a strange calm in my spirit. It was as if God had gathered every tear and turned them into prayers I did not have the strength to say. Slowly, the sharp edges of my pain began to soften. The same waves that once knocked me down began to carry me forward.

One of the most important lessons I learned was that God is not disappointed by our emotions. He is not impatient when we stumble through our healing. He meets us right where we are. On the good days, He rejoices with us. On the hard days, He holds us closer. The truth is, some of the most sacred work happens in the in-between spaces, when we are still fragile, still uncertain, but still choosing to believe that restoration is coming.

Every setback became an invitation to return to His presence. Every valley taught me something about His faithfulness. Healing, I realized, is not about reaching a destination where everything is perfect. It is about walking hand in hand with the One who never leaves us.

So if you find yourself taking two steps forward and one step back, do not lose heart. You are still moving, even if it feels slow. Every tear, every prayer, every quiet act of faith is shaping you into something more substantial and more beautiful. Healing is not linear because God's work in you is not rushed. It unfolds in His perfect timing, one moment of grace at a time.

The Gentle Work of God

Healing did not arrive with fireworks or fanfare. It did not come through a sudden revelation or a dramatic encounter. It came quietly, in gentle waves, almost unnoticed at first. One morning, I realized I had gone several days without crying. Another day, I caught myself humming a song while cooking. Those little moments were not loud, but they were sacred. They were proof that God was working tenderly and consistently in the background of my heart.

The gentle work of God does not rush. He does not demand that we skip over our pain or pretend that it no longer exists. Instead, He meets us in the middle of it. He sits with us in the quiet, steadying our breathing, softening our hearts, and reminding us that His presence is not dependent on our performance. I used to think that healing would happen when I felt strong again. What I learned is that healing begins when I let God be strong for me.

There were still days when old memories resurfaced like waves hitting the shore. Sometimes the ache would return unexpectedly—a song, a photograph, or a scent would take me back to a place I was trying to forget. But this time, I noticed something different. The memories no longer crushed me. They passed through like soft rain instead of a storm. I could acknowledge the pain, feel it for a moment, and then let it go. That was grace in motion.

One of the ways God began to restore me was through stillness. I learned that silence is not empty when God fills it. In those quiet moments of prayer, I stopped trying to find all the answers and started listening. The world teaches us to chase healing as if it were a prize to be earned. But God whispered to me, "Be still, and know that I am God." That knowing changed everything.

In stillness, He reminded me that my worth was not tied to being a wife, a mother, or anyone's anchor. My value was not determined by who stayed or who left. It was rooted in Him. The more I sat in His presence, the more I felt layers of shame and regret peel away. It was as if God was gently rebuilding me from the inside out, not in haste but with careful love.

The gentle work of God often shows up through people, too. A friend who calls to check in. A sermon that feels like it was written just for you. A stranger's smile on a day you felt invisible. These are not coincidences. They are reminders that God weaves healing into the fabric of our everyday lives.

One afternoon, I was sitting by the water, watching the waves roll in. The sky was painted with soft hues of pink and gold, and the breeze felt like a quiet embrace. As I watched the ripples stretch across the lake, I heard that familiar whisper again: "See, I make all things new." The words from **Revelation 21:5** settled deep in my spirit. God was not only healing what was broken; He was creating something entirely new out of my pain.

That realization brought peace. I began to see that the gentle work of God is not about returning to who you were before the hurt. It is about becoming someone new through His grace. The cracks in your heart do not disqualify you. They make you more compassionate, more patient, and more aware of the beauty that can grow from ashes.

Healing became a partnership between my willingness and God's power. Each time I surrendered another piece of my story to Him, the anger, the disappointment, the unanswered questions: He exchanged it for something better. Sometimes it was peace. Sometimes it was clarity. Sometimes it was simply the strength to keep going. But he always gave something in return.

I also began to notice that God was using my story to touch others. Friends and even strangers would share their struggles, and I could say with conviction, "You will make it through this." Not because I read it somewhere, but because I had lived it. That is the beauty of God's gentle work. He turns your scars into stories that bring hope to others.

There is a passage in Isaiah 61 that says God will give us "beauty for ashes, the oil of joy for mourning, and a garment of praise for the spirit of heaviness." I have lived that promise. The ashes of my brokenness became the soil where new life began to grow. The joy that returned was not the same as before. It was deeper, steadier, rooted in gratitude for the One who had walked with me through the fire and brought me out refined.

Now, when I look back, I no longer see only what was lost. I see what was gained: strength I did not know I had, compassion I could not have learned any other way, and faith that has become unshakable. I see a woman who is not defined by her pain, but refined by God's love.

The gentle work of God is not always visible at first. It begins in secret places, in whispers, in small acts of surrender. But over time, it becomes evident in how you speak, how you love, and how you live. It transforms not only your circumstances, but your very soul.

So if your healing feels slow, take heart. You are not behind. You are right on schedule with the pace of God's grace. He is still working, still shaping, restoring. And one day, you will look back and see that even in your quietest moments, He was building something beautiful within you.

A.R.E. in Action

This is where my A.R.E. principle moved from theory to practice.

- **Acknowledge:** I admitted I was hurting and not pretending, and I was not covering it up. I journaled my rawest emotions. Some pages were soaked with tears, but that honesty became the first step in God's healing work.

- **Release:** I began letting go of resentment, fear, and bitterness. Not all at once, but little by little. Each prayer where I whispered, "Lord, I give this to You," lightened my load.

- **Empower:** Each act of self-care, prayer, and trust gave me back a piece of my strength. Walking, eating better, spending time in worship, they were not just habits; they were declarations that I was choosing life over despair.

Teachable Moment: Small Steps Lead to Big Healing

We often underestimate the power of small steps. We look for significant breakthroughs but often overlook the quiet victories. Getting out of bed, calling a friend, or opening your Bible may not feel like much, but in God's eyes, those steps are sacred.

Think about the story of Elijah in 1 Kings 19. After a great victory, he ran into the wilderness, exhausted and ready to give up. He prayed for God to take his life. Instead of rebuking him, God sent an angel who told him to eat and rest. God did not demand that Elijah be strong in that moment. He asked him to take the next small step: eat, rest, rise. Healing often begins with something as simple as nourishment, rest, and one obedient step forward.

The Discipline of Journaling

One of the tools that helped me most was journaling. Writing became a safe place to release what I could not always say out loud. Some entries were filled with anger. Others were laced with regret. Many were so raw I could not read them back without tears. But each page reminded me that I was no longer bottling it up.

Journaling became a prayer in itself. Even when I didn't know what to pray, the act of putting pen to paper allowed my soul to find its voice. And often, as I wrote, I would feel the Holy Spirit reminding me of scriptures or whispering comfort into the margins of my sorrow.

If you are walking through your own healing, I encourage you to write. Do not worry about perfect sentences or grammar. Let your journal be a place where you can acknowledge the storm inside you without fear of judgment.

Practical Tool: Create a Healing Plan

Choose one action for your body, one for your mind, and one for your spirit. Commit to these three for seven days and track your progress.

- **Body:** Nourish yourself with rest, healthy food, or gentle movement. Even a ten-minute walk can shift your perspective.

- **Mind:** Replace negative loops with affirmations or scripture memorization. Let God's truth be louder than the lies of regret.

- **Spirit:** Spend intentional time in prayer, worship, or journaling. Even a few minutes can center you in God's presence.

Healing is not about perfection. It is about consistency. After seven days, review how these small actions shifted your perspective. You may not see a radical transformation in a week, but you will notice that your spirit feels lighter and your hope stronger.

Relearning Joy

One of the surprising parts of healing was rediscovering joy in simple things. I had believed that joy was tied to circumstances, that I would only feel it again once everything in my life was put back together. But slowly, I began to experience joy in unexpected ways.

I found joy in laughter that bubbled up during a phone call with my children. I found joy in cooking a meal that actually turned out right. I found joy in singing along to worship music while cleaning my kitchen.

Nehemiah 8:10 says, *"The joy of the Lord is your strength."* That verse became real to me during this season. Joy was not something I had to create; it was something I had to discover. It was a gift God gave me, and it became strength for my weary soul.

Reflection Exercise

- What emotions or memories do I need to acknowledge right now?

- What burden am I ready to release into God's hands today?

- What small action can I take to empower myself to step toward healing this week?

Take time to write your answers. Do not rush. Let the Holy Spirit guide you as you reflect.

Daily Affirmations

Speak these over yourself each morning this week:

1. Each small step I take is moving me toward healing.

2. I trust God to restore what has been broken.

3. I release resentment and choose peace today.

4. My strength is not in myself but in the Lord who sustains me.

5. God's joy gives me strength for every season.

A Story of Hope

During one of my speaking engagements, a woman approached me with tears in her eyes. She shared that after her own divorce, she could not imagine life ever feeling normal again. She told me she would lie in bed for hours, too heavy with grief to move. One day, she decided to start with one small step. She got out of bed, opened her Bible, and read just one verse. That small act became a turning point. It did not erase her pain, but it reminded her that God was still with her.

Her testimony echoed my own journey. Healing rarely comes in dramatic moments. It begins in ordinary, quiet choices. One verse. One prayer. One walk. One laugh. And over time, those moments stitch together into a tapestry of restoration.

Prayer

Lord, thank You for being my Healer. I acknowledge the pain I carry, but I also release it into Your hands. Empower me to take small steps toward restoration and to trust that You are making me whole again. Thank you for reminding me that joy can return, even in the small things. Teach me to celebrate progress, no matter how slow it seems. Help me believe that the story you are writing in my life is not over. In Jesus' name, Amen.

Closing Thought

Healing does not always arrive with fanfare. It often begins in the quiet, ordinary choices of each day. One step at a time, God pieces us back together; not just as we were before, but stronger, wiser, and ready to walk in the fullness of His purpose.

Remember this: your small steps matter. They are sacred in God's eyes. Do not despise the days of small beginnings. Trust that each step is carrying you closer to the restoration He has promised.

4.

SACRED PAUSE

Relocating back to my home country was not part of my original plan. It felt like retreating. I wondered what people would think of me. Would they assume I had failed? Would they whisper that I was running away? For a time, those questions haunted me. I replayed them in my mind, almost hearing imaginary voices of judgment. In my weakest moments, I began to agree with those voices. Maybe I had failed. Maybe I was running.

But in the quiet of that season, I discovered something unexpected. God had designed it as a sacred pause. I needed distance from the noise, the questions, and the expectations of others. I needed space to be with Him and face myself.

Being alone was something I had never experienced before. I had always lived in a cocoon of family. I had parents, siblings, a husband, and children. I was always someone's wife, someone's mother, someone's caretaker. Now, for the first time, it was just me. The silence felt foreign at first, almost threatening. Yet, in time, I discovered that the silence also held space for something new. Sometimes you have to move away from the noise and places of familiarity to regain your strength. That was me, needing to find me again. I love the song that says, *"Silence the noise in my mind, Lord, and open the eyes of my heart. I want to hear you."*

At first, the stillness made me restless. I did not know

what to do with the quiet. I filled my days with small tasks to feel productive, organizing my kitchen, washing dishes that were already clean, and folding and refolding laundry. My apartment was spotless. It took me a while to realize that God was inviting me to stop doing and start being. He was calling me to rediscover who I was without all the roles and titles.

There were moments when I sat by the window, watching the sunlight spill across the floor, and I felt tears well up for no apparent reason. Those tears were not just from sadness; they were from release. It was as if my soul was exhaling after years of holding its breath. In those still moments, I began to hear God's voice more clearly. He was not condemning me for my mistakes or failures. Instead, I felt His gentle reassurance: "You are still mine. You are not forgotten. You are not finished."

I began to understand that solitude is not punishment; it is preparation. God uses quiet seasons to restore what chaos has broken. The silence became a classroom where I learned to listen again, to Him, to my own heart, and to the rhythms of grace that had always been there but often drowned out by noise.

In that space of solitude, I began to journal every night. I poured out my thoughts, prayers, and questions onto paper. Some entries were full of pain and confusion. Others were whispers of hope, small glimpses of healing. Writing became a form of prayer, a way of processing all that was shifting inside me.

There were nights when I played soft worship music on the radio and sat in God's presence, even left it on all night. I did not have fancy prayers, only simple words: "Lord, heal me." And somehow, in those unspoken moments, He did. Not all at once, but piece by piece.

Returning home was never about running away. It was

about returning to the place where God could meet me again. I had to step away from the world that knew me by my past so that I could rediscover the woman God was shaping me to become.

Looking back, I realize that what felt like a retreat was actually a repositioning. God was not moving me backward; He was realigning me. He took me out of the noise so that He could tune my Spirit to His frequency.

That season of solitude became the soil where healing began to grow. It was uncomfortable, yes, but it was also holy. Sometimes God brings us to quiet places not to isolate us, but to prepare us for the next chapter. The silence I once feared became the very thing that taught me how to hear again: not the voices of judgment or regret, but the voice of my Father saying, "Be still, daughter. You are safe with me."

Life in Tunapuna

I rented an apartment in Tunapuna, Trinidad. It was not large or fancy, but it became my refuge. The walls were simple, the rooms modest, yet there was something sacred about that small space. I ensured it was gated for my protection because security gave me a sense of control when everything else in life felt wildly uncertain. Within those gates, I could breathe. I could cry without judgment. I could rebuild without anyone watching.

I found a job at a medical lab and later worked part-time at a clothing store. The work kept me occupied and gave me a reason to get out of bed in the morning. Something was healing about having a purpose again, even if it was small. Earning my own income reminded me that I was still capable, still useful, still standing.

I made a few friends along the way, but I kept my circle small. I was careful about who I allowed into my space because I was still fragile, still learning how to protect my peace. On Christmas Day, my friends Petra and Fitzroy came by, bringing laughter and conversation that filled the air for a few precious hours. My aunt also visited frequently, and her presence felt like a warm blanket on cold days. Beyond that, I preferred solitude. For the first time in my life, I did not want a house full of noise. I wanted stillness.

In the evenings, I would make a cup of tea, sit by the window, and listen to the sounds of the neighbourhood, the dogs barking in the distance, the faint rhythm of soca music from a nearby radio, the chatter of people passing by on the street below. Those sounds reminded me that life was continuing all around me, even as mine felt paused.

I spent many nights crying and journaling. God was the only one who truly knew how I was doing. To others, I wore the polite smile, the professional face, the mask that said, "I'm fine." But behind closed doors, I wrestled with grief that would not let go. Journaling became my outlet, my confession, and my conversation with God. I would pour out my heart in long, messy sentences, sometimes ending with nothing more than the words, "Help me, Lord."

And somehow, He always did. The more I wrote, the more I began to see patterns, moments of gratitude hidden within the pain, little reminders that I was not as alone as I felt.

When the heaviness became too much, I would take short trips to Tobago. The first time I stepped off the ferry, I felt a peace I had not felt in years. The island seemed to breathe differently. The air was softer, the pace slower. The beaches stretched out like God's open arms. The sound of the waves became my therapy. The ocean had a way of speaking to me without words.

I would sit for hours, watching the tide roll in and out,

and it felt as if God was washing away the remnants of my sorrow with every wave. I would whisper prayers into the wind, letting them drift across the water. The horizon reminded me of hope. Even when I could not see what was beyond it, I knew it was there.

Those trips became my personal retreats, moments of sacred rest for my soul. I did not go there to escape life but to reconnect with it. The quiet gave me room to think, to forgive, and to breathe again. I would return to Tunapuna lighter each time, carrying with me the peace that only God and the sea could give.

Looking back now, I see that my small apartment and those island visits were more than just a season of recovery. They were a season of preparation. God was using that quiet place to rebuild my foundation, one prayer, one tear, and one wave at a time.

The Beach as a Sanctuary

I would sit for hours, watching the waves crash against the shore as if God Himself was washing away my shame with every tide. The rhythmic sound of the water was both soothing and strong, steady as a heartbeat, reminding me that life was still pulsing around me even when I felt numb inside. Sometimes I cried until I had no more tears left, and other times I sat in silence, staring at the horizon, waiting for peace to come. Slowly, it did.

My aunt Ann became my companion in those moments. She was walking through her own storm, having gone through a divorce as well. There was an unspoken understanding between us, a quiet sisterhood of two women rediscovering who they were outside of the titles they once carried. We would take the short flight from Trinidad to Tobago, carrying only light bags, just enough for the weekend. Once we arrived, we would drop our things off at the villa and jump into a van headed straight for Store Bay.

The drive there always made me feel like I was shedding something. The closer we got to the beach, the lighter I felt. The sight of palm trees swaying gently in the breeze and the smell of salt in the air felt like a promise of peace. Tobago had a way of embracing you, as if the island itself whispered, "You are safe here."

Ann and I spent hours on the sand, sometimes talking, sometimes saying nothing at all. We shared our stories over fresh mangoes, fried plantains, and the rich flavours of Tobago cuisine that tasted like comfort and home. There was healing in those simple pleasures. The act of eating together, laughing at old memories, and feeling the warm sun on our faces reminded us that joy was still possible.

The beach became more than a getaway; it became a sacred place where God met us both. The sound of the waves became a form of prayer. The wind carried away words we could not say out loud. Every ripple across the water seemed to reflect His mercy. When the tide came in, it felt like grace arriving all over again.

Nature has a way of speaking God's truth without words. Each wave reminded me of renewal. Each sunrise testified that no night lasts forever. Each seabird, rising and falling on the wind, reminded me that life continues even after storms. I began to pay attention to the small details: the shimmer of the sunlight on the water, the way the sand felt cool beneath my feet early in the morning, and the rhythm of the waves that seemed to match the cadence of my heartbeat.

It was during one of those mornings, sitting quietly on Store Bay's shore, that I finally felt the weight of guilt begin to lift. I realized that I had spent so much time reliving my mistakes that I had forgotten to receive God's mercy. The ocean reminded me of that mercy: vast, unending, and more profound than anything I could comprehend.

I began to see the connection between the ocean's rhythm and God's character. The waves did not stop coming, just as His grace does not stop flowing. The tides may rise and fall, but they always return. So does His love. Each morning, I watched the sunlight stretch across the water and thought, "If creation can begin again every day, so can I."

The beach became my place of surrender. It was where I laid down my regrets, one by one, and let the waves carry them away. It was where I found stillness, not just around me but within me. And it was where I learned that healing does not always happen in the noise of doing but in the quiet of being.

By the time Ann and I would pack up to return to Trinidad, I always felt renewed. My skin smelled of salt, my hair tangled with the breeze, and my heart a little lighter than before. The peace of Tobago stayed with me long after I left its shores. It was as if the sea had written its own prayer across my Spirit, one that said, "You are being made whole."

The Power of Stillness

In that pause, I began to notice things I had ignored for years. The pace of my life had been so loud and demanding that I rarely stopped to be. I had been so busy doing, helping, fixing, and caring for others that I had forgotten how to exist in God's presence simply. Returning home gave me the gift of stillness. It was uncomfortable at first. I was not used to being alone with my thoughts. Silence magnified everything I had buried. It echoed the memories I tried so hard to suppress and brought to the surface the emotions I had carefully tucked away. But over time, I came to see the stillness as an invitation, not a punishment.

At first, I tried to fill the quiet. I turned on the television for background noise. I played music to avoid hearing my own thoughts. But the Spirit kept calling me back to the quiet. It was in that silence that I realized how much noise I had allowed to define my life. For years, I had moved from one responsibility to another without stopping to ask, "How is my soul?" The stillness stripped away the distractions. It forced me to face the woman in the mirror and meet her with grace rather than judgment.

I found myself journaling more than ever before. Page after page, I poured out my heart to God. Some entries were filled with anger that I had buried under busyness. Others exposed regret I could not let go of. Many were blurred with tears that stained the paper. Yet in that broken honesty, something remarkable happened. I stopped performing for God and began conversing with Him. My prayers became less about asking and more about listening. I started to see that stillness is not the absence of movement; it is the presence of peace.

In those quiet moments, I began to hear God's voice in ways I never had before. It was not a booming shout. It was not a sermon or a prophecy. It was a whisper reminding me, "Daughter, you are still Mine. I forgive you. Now, forgive yourself."

Those words echoed through my Spirit like waves crashing against the rocks. They did not erase my past, but they reframed it. I was still His. No mistake had changed that. The more time I spent in His presence, the more I began to understand that God's silence is not His absence. It is often His invitation to come closer.

One night, I remember sitting with my journal open and whispering, "Lord, what are You doing in me?" The answer came quietly but firmly: "I am teaching you how to rest." That answer brought me to tears. I had not realized how exhausted I was, not just physically, but emotionally and spiritually. I had been running on empty for years, trying to prove my worth through what I did for others. In the stillness, God was teaching me that my worth was not in doing but in being His daughter.

As I leaned into the quiet, I began to notice small things that once went unseen: the sound of rain on the roof, the way sunlight filtered through my curtains in the morning, the sweet chorus of birds outside my window. Each sound and sight became a gentle reminder that God was present in the ordinary. I started to understand ***Psalm 46:10 in a new way: "Be still, and know that I am God."***

Stillness became my teacher. It taught me patience when I wanted to rush the healing process. It taught me to listen more than I speak. It taught me that peace is not found in the absence of pain, but in the presence of God within it.

In that sacred quiet, I found renewal. My heart, once heavy with noise and striving, began to rest in the truth that God's love was constant and unchanging. The stillness did not erase my story; it helped me see it through His eyes—redeemed, forgiven, and loved beyond measure.

Wrestling With Self-Forgiveness

Self-forgiveness is often harder than forgiving others. We can extend grace to those who have hurt us and still refuse to extend that same grace to ourselves. We hold ourselves hostage to regret, replaying mistakes over and over, punishing ourselves with endless "if only" questions.

If only I had seen the signs sooner.

If only I had prayed harder.

If only I had been different.

If only I had made another choice.

Those thoughts can become chains that tighten every time we replay the past. We relive conversations, decisions, and moments that cannot be changed. We tell ourselves that we should have known better, done better, been better. Long after others have moved on, we stay imprisoned by guilt that God has already released.

For a long time, that was me. I knew all the scriptures about forgiveness, and I believed them for everyone else. I could tell another woman that God's grace covers her mistakes, that His mercy is new every morning. But when it came to myself, I struggled to believe that same truth applied. I felt disqualified. I thought I had disappointed God beyond repair.

Every time I prayed, my mind whispered reminders of what I had done wrong. Even when I was smiling on the outside, an inner voice kept saying, "You are not enough." It was as if I were carrying a heavy backpack filled with every mistake I had ever made, dragging it into every new day. I could not find the strength to put it down.

Then one afternoon, while sitting on the beach, I finally stopped running from the quiet. The sea was calm that day, the waves gentle, the air still. I sat on the warm sand and whispered, "God, I do not know how to forgive myself. Please teach me."

It was not a thunderous moment. There were no lightning flashes or dramatic signs. But I felt His presence wrap around me like a warm blanket. It was quiet, steady, and undeniable. It was as if God Himself was sitting beside me, whispering to my weary soul, "You are already forgiven."

I realized in that moment that the problem was not that God had withheld forgiveness. He had extended it long ago. I was the one refusing to accept it. I had mistaken guilt for humility, as if punishing myself somehow proved my sincerity. But God never asked me to carry what He had already carried to the cross.

Tears streamed down my face as I let those words sink in. I whispered back, "So I can let this go?" And in my Spirit, I heard, "Yes, daughter. Let it go. You cannot heal while holding on to what I have already washed away."

That realization changed everything. It did not erase my past, but it reframed it. My failures were not the end of my story. They were the soil from which growth would come. The same grace that forgave me was now calling me to live free.

Forgiving myself became an act of faith. Each time guilt tried to return, I had to remind myself, "I am forgiven." Sometimes I said it out loud until my heart began to believe it. I learned that forgiveness is not a feeling. It is a choice. Feelings eventually follow the choice, but the choice must come first.

Romans 8:1 became a cornerstone for my healing: "There is therefore now no condemnation for those who are in Christ Jesus." Those words were a lifeline. They reminded me that condemnation was not God's voice. It was the enemy's echo, trying to drag me back into shame. God's voice always leads to restoration, never accusation.

That day on the beach marked a turning point. I left the shore lighter than I had arrived. I could almost feel the weight of regret slipping into the waves, carried far beyond reach. I realized that accepting God's forgiveness is not arrogance; it is obedience. It is saying yes to His mercy and no to the lies that keep us bound.

From that moment on, every sunrise over the water reminded me of His faithfulness. Each wave that touched the sand felt like another whisper from heaven saying, "You are free."

The Freedom of No Condemnation

Romans 8:1 says, "Therefore, there is now no condemnation for those who are in Christ Jesus."

Those words broke something inside me. They cut through years of guilt and striving. They reminded me that condemnation was not God's voice. It was the enemy's. For too long, I had confused conviction with condemnation. Conviction draws you closer to God, but condemnation pushes you away. Conviction says, "You can begin again." Condemnation says, "You will never change." One brings healing. The other brings despair.

As I sat with that scripture, I began to see that God was never the one rehearsing my failures. He does not sit in heaven replaying my mistakes or shaking His head at my weakness. That is not His nature. He redeems what is broken. He restores what is lost. He does not keep a record of wrongs; He blots them out with His mercy. He is not keeping score. He is keeping promises.

That truth began to dismantle the walls I had built around my heart. For years, I thought I had to earn God's approval, to prove through perfection that I was still worthy of love. But grace reminded me that I never had to earn what was already given to me. God's love had been there all along, waiting for me to stop hiding behind shame.

For the first time, I believed that my past failures did not disqualify me from God's love or His purpose. My mistakes did not cancel my calling. They became part of the testimony that revealed God's grace. Forgiving myself was not about excusing what had happened. It was about releasing the burden of shame and aligning with God's truth rather than the enemy's lies.

That shift changed how I saw everything. I began to walk with a new kind of peace. I no longer carried the invisible weight of guilt that had followed me for years. I stopped apologizing for my existence and started thanking

God for my redemption. Each morning, I reminded myself of this truth: "I am not my past. I am His daughter."

That season by the sea became the birthplace of true healing. It did not happen overnight. Healing rarely does. It came step by step, tear by tear, prayer by prayer. Each time I walked away from the shoreline, I felt lighter than when I arrived. I carried not shame, but hope.

The waves became a reflection of grace itself: steady, constant, cleansing. Every time the tide rolled in, it felt as though God was whispering, "See, I make all things new." And I began to believe Him.

There were still moments when old memories tried to rise again, when guilt tried to creep back in like the evening tide. But instead of giving in to it, I spoke the truth out loud: "There is no condemnation for me because I am in Christ." Saying it aloud became a declaration of freedom. It reminded both my heart and the enemy that I was no longer bound to my past.

As time went on, I noticed how that freedom began to change how I related to others. I could extend more grace because I was finally living in grace myself. I could look at my scars and see them not as proof of failure, but as evidence of survival. God had turned every wound into a story of His mercy.

I learned that freedom is not the absence of pain. It is the presence of peace that comes when you know you are forgiven and loved beyond measure. It is waking up each day and choosing to walk in that truth, no matter what yesterday looked like.

Every trip to the beach became a reminder of this promise. The waves would come and go, but God's love remained the same. The ocean, vast and unending, mirrored His mercy: deep, boundless, and consistently enough.

When I left Tobago and returned home, I carried that peace with me. It was no longer just a place I visited. It became a state of being. The freedom I found was not in geography. It was in grace.

A Teachable Story

One afternoon in Tobago, I watched a fisherman pull his small boat onto the shore. The boat was weathered, scratched, and scarred by storms. Yet it was still afloat, still serving its purpose. The fisherman did not see the scars as proof of failure. They were proof that the boat had endured.

God showed me that I was like that boat. I carried scars, yes, but they were not signs of disqualification. They were signs of survival. My story, marked by loss and regret, could still serve His purpose. My life, scarred as it was, was still valuable in His hands.

A.R.E. Focus: Release Shame and Regret

When I returned home from that sacred time by the sea, I carried more than memories of the beach. I carried a new understanding of grace. I had spent so many years carrying guilt like a heavy backpack, but now I began to realize that God never intended for me to live weighed down by shame. He wanted me to live free.

Shame and regret are heavy companions. They whisper lies that sound convincing. They tell you that you are unworthy, that you have missed your chance, that your mistakes define your destiny. For years, I believed those lies. I tried to earn back approval through perfection, through performance, through proving myself. But all that striving only made me more tired and more disconnected from the truth of who I was in Christ.

Freedom began when I chose to face those lies with honesty. I sat with my journal and wrote down the moments that still made me wince; the ones I avoided thinking about because they carried so much pain. I wrote down the words

I wished I had not said, the decisions I wished I had made differently, and the times I failed to love myself or others well. It wasn't easy, but it was necessary. I realized that until I acknowledged those moments, I could never let them go.

The A.R.E. principle: Acknowledge, Release, Empoweris more than a concept. It became the roadmap God used to rebuild my heart.

Acknowledge: I stopped pretending I was fine. I admitted that I was hurt, ashamed, and still healing. I brought my truth before God, trusting that He could handle it. Acknowledgment does not make you weak. It makes you honest.

Release: Once I had named the pain, I began to surrender it in prayer. Sometimes that meant crying through every word. Sometimes it meant sitting quietly and simply saying, "Lord, I give this to You." Release is not a one-time act. It is a process. It means choosing every day not to pick up what you have already laid at God's feet.

Empower: The final step was learning to walk in freedom. Empowerment is not pride; it is confidence rooted in grace. It is living like someone who knows she has been forgiven. It is speaking life over yourself instead of rehearsing failure. It is believed that God can still use your story for good, even the parts you once wanted to erase.

Each part of this process required courage. There were days when I felt like I was making progress and days when I slipped back into old patterns of thinking. But even on the hard days, I kept choosing to return to the truth. I reminded myself that forgiveness is not a feeling. It is a decision to live aligned with God's mercy rather than your mistakes.

Releasing shame and regret is like unclenching your fists after years of holding on too tightly. At first, it hurts.

Your hands ache from being stuck in that position for so long. But then the blood starts to flow again, and you realize how much lighter you feel.

God began to fill those open hands with peace. He reminded me that His grace is greater than my guilt and that His love has no expiration date. Every time I caught myself rehearsing regret, I would whisper, "It is finished." That is what Jesus said on the cross. Those three words hold the power to silence shame forever.

Practical Tool: The Self-Forgiveness Letter

If you struggle to let go of your own mistakes, try this exercise. Take time this week to write a letter to yourself as if you were writing to a dear friend. Offer compassion. Speak words of grace. Acknowledge the pain but release the blame.

Begin your letter by saying:
"I forgive you for the times you did not know better. I forgive you for trying to be everything to everyone and losing yourself in the process. I forgive you for carrying burdens that were never yours to hold. I forgive you for believing that one season of failure could cancel a lifetime of purpose."

When you are done, read the letter aloud. Then, if you feel led, tear it up or place it in your Bible as a reminder that those burdens now belong to God. End by affirming:
"I am forgiven. I am free. I am loved."

Reflection Exercise

- What memories or regrets still carry shame for me?

- What scripture can I declare over myself when guilt rises again?

- How can I create a "sanctuary space" where I meet God in stillness, just as I did on the beach?

Daily Affirmations

I am not condemned. I am forgiven in Christ.
My past does not define my future.
God's mercy is greater than my mistakes.
I release shame and choose freedom today.

Prayer

Lord, thank You for Your mercy that never fails. Help me release the weight of regret and forgive myself, as You have already forgiven me. When guilt rises, remind me of Your truth that I am free in Christ and worthy of love. Teach me to walk each day lighter, carrying hope instead of shame. In Jesus' name, Amen.

Closing Thought

Forgiving yourself is not a weakness. It is courage. It takes strength to face the past and choose freedom. The sacred pauses in life, though uncomfortable, are often where God whispers His loudest truths. In stillness, shame is washed away, and hope rises like the tide.

5.

THE MOUNTAIN OF FORGIVENESS

Forgiving myself was only part of the journey. The next mountain to climb was forgiving the one who had broken my heart. I wish I could tell you it was easy, that one prayer swept away years of pain and replaced it with instant peace. But forgiveness is not a switch you flip. It is a choice you make over and over again until your heart finally catches up with your decision.

For a long time, I resisted. The very thought of forgiving felt unfair. Why should I forgive someone who had caused me so much pain? It felt like letting him off the hook, like saying the betrayal and the broken promises did not matter. I told myself that forgiveness would mean I had minimized the hurt, or worse, excused it. My heart was not ready to take that step, and I held on tightly to my right to be angry.

Anger felt powerful at first. It made me feel in control when everything else had been taken from me. But that control was an illusion. The truth is, anger burns bright, but it burns you, too. The longer I held on to it, the heavier it became. What I did not realize at first was that unforgiveness was not chaining him; it was chaining me. Every time I replayed the past in my mind, I was handing my peace over to him all over again. He was not losing sleep because of my resentment, but I was.

Unforgiveness built invisible walls around my heart. It blocked the flow of joy, love, and even prayer. I would try to worship, but my mind would drift back to what was done to me. I would try to pray, but bitterness would rise like a wall between me and the words I wanted to say. I began to realize that unforgiveness does not just affect your emotions. It affects your Spirit. It cuts you off from the very healing you are asking God to bring.

There came a day when I could no longer carry the weight. I remember sitting at my kitchen table with tears streaming down my face, saying aloud, "God, I do not want to forgive. I do not feel like forgiving. But I cannot live like this anymore." That was the first honest prayer I had prayed about it. And I believe that is precisely where forgiveness begins, not in perfection, but in surrender.

In that moment, I sensed the gentle whisper of the Holy Spirit reminding me that forgiveness was not about fairness. It was about freedom. Fairness looks for repayment. Freedom releases it. God was not asking me to excuse what had been done. He was asking me to trust Him with the outcome.

I began to understand that forgiveness is not an event. It is a journey. Sometimes it starts with clenched fists and ends with open hands. It begins when you decide, even through tears, to let God do what only He can do. Some days, I could say, "I forgive," and feel a small sense of relief. Other days, I had to repeat it again and again, even when the pain resurfaced. Forgiveness is a process of pruning the soul. You cut away resentment little by little until only peace remains.

What changed me most was realizing that forgiveness does not depend on the other person's apology. It is a gift you give to yourself and to God. When you forgive, you are not saying the hurt was acceptable. You are saying it no longer has authority over your life. You are releasing your right to revenge and placing justice into the hands of a God who sees and knows all things.

Each time I chose forgiveness, the hold of bitterness weakened. My heart began to feel lighter. I could breathe again. The memories did not disappear; they lost their power to wound me. I learned that true forgiveness does not erase the past. It reclaims the present. It gives you back your peace, your joy, and your freedom to move forward.

Forgiveness was never really about him deserving it. Forgiveness was about me needing it. It was about saying, "Lord, I trust You with what I cannot fix. I release this so you can restore me."

The Turning Point

There was a day I sat with my Bible open, weary from the battle inside me. My heart felt like a battlefield: hope on one side, resentment on the other. I had prayed for healing, but what I really wanted was justice. I wanted God to see how deeply I had been wronged and to make the other person feel the pain I had carried for years. Yet even as those thoughts rose in me, another voice spoke quietly through the noise of my anger.

My eyes fell on ***Matthew 6:14: "For if you forgive other people when they sin against you, your heavenly Father will also forgive you."***

I reread it. Then again. Those words pierced me in a way I could not ignore. Forgiveness was not a suggestion. It was not a topic for debate. It was a command: a sacred act of obedience. But more than that, it was also a gift. By forgiving, I was not excusing sin; I was choosing freedom.

At first, that truth made me angry. How could God ask me to forgive when my heart still ached so deeply? I wanted to move forward, but every reminder of betrayal reopened the wound. I could forgive in theory, but living it out was another story. Forgiveness felt like surrendering justice. It felt like saying, "What happened was acceptable," when it was not. But the Spirit kept pressing on my heart: forgiveness does not mean agreement; it means Release.

I wrestled with that verse for weeks. I would close my Bible and whisper, "God, You do not know how much it hurts." But I knew He did. Every time I brought my pain to Him, He did not scold me. He listened. He waited patiently for my heart to soften.

I cried until I was hoarse. I paced the floor late at night, praying and arguing all at once. Forgiveness felt too costly. It felt impossible. But deep inside, I knew I had reached a crossroads. I could either hold on to bitterness or walk the path toward peace. Both were choices. One left me trapped in a cycle of pain. The other led me into healing.

I remember the exact moment I whispered the words for the first time: "God, I choose to forgive." It was not a loud declaration. It was quiet and trembling, like a fragile seed planted in hard soil. But that seed was the beginning of freedom. I did not feel peace immediately, but something shifted in my Spirit. The wall I had built between myself and God began to crack. His presence, which had felt distant, drew near again.

Forgiveness was not a one-time act for me. It was a daily surrender. Some mornings, I had to repeat it before I could even face the day. Other times, I would be driving in my car, and an old memory would surface, bringing with it a familiar sting. In those moments, I would take a deep breath and whisper, "Lord, I still choose to forgive." Each time I did, the pain lost a little more power over me.

Eventually, I began to realize that forgiveness was less about forgetting and more about freedom. It was not about pretending the pain never happened. It was about choosing not to live in that pain anymore. God was teaching me that forgiveness was the doorway through which healing walked in.

The day I finally surrendered completely, I felt peace for the first time in years. It was not loud or dramatic. It was still, gentle, and deeply personal like a warm sunrise breaking over a long night. That peace did not come because everything was fixed. It came because my heart was finally free.

When I look back now, I see that forgiveness was never meant to make the other person comfortable. It was meant to make me whole.

Forgiveness as a Daily Choice

I wish I could say that once I decided to forgive, everything changed overnight. I wanted to wake up the next morning completely free of pain, with no memories that hurt and no thoughts that made my chest tighten. But forgiveness does not work that way. It is not an event; it is a process. It must be chosen again and again, sometimes every single day.

There were mornings I woke up feeling strong and at peace, convinced that the past no longer had a hold on me. Then something would happen, a song would play, a name would appear on social media, or a memory would resurface—and suddenly the pain would return like a wave. In those moments, I had to remind myself that forgiveness was not a feeling. It was a decision I had already made, one I would keep making until my heart caught up with it.

Each time I felt the sting of anger, I would whisper, "Lord, I forgive again." At first, it felt repetitive, almost mechanical, but over time, those words became powerful. They were my declaration that the past no longer had permission to rule my present. Each time I spoke to them, I took back a little more of my peace.

Some days, I did not even have the strength to say it out loud. On those days, I would sit quietly and pray for God to fill the space where resentment wanted to grow. Sometimes forgiveness looked like tears on my pillow and silence in my prayers. Other times, it looked like singing along to worship music through gritted teeth, asking God to heal what still hurt.

Forgiveness became an act of faith. It meant trusting that God's justice was enough. It meant releasing my desire for revenge and believing that God could handle what I could not. Romans 12:19 reminded me of this truth: "Do not take revenge, my dear friends, but leave room for God's wrath, for it is written: 'It is mine to avenge; I will repay,' says the Lord."

That verse brought both conviction and comfort. It told me I didn't have to fix everything. I did not have to make the other person see what they had done or feel what I had felt. That was God's work, not mine. My job was to stay free, to guard my peace, and to keep walking forward.

It took time, but slowly I began to notice a change. My prayers shifted. At first, they were filled with pain and pleading, asking God to change the situation, to bring justice, to make things right. But eventually, those prayers softened into something new. I began to pray for his well-being. I began to ask God to bless him, to help him grow, and to draw him closer to Himself. That was when I knew forgiveness had done its work in me.

It did not mean we became close again. Forgiveness does not always lead to reconciliation. It does not mean you forget or return to a place of hurt. What it means is that you are no longer carrying the poison in your own heart. Forgiveness releases you to live again. It permits you to breathe, to smile, and to move forward without the heavy weight of bitterness holding you down.

Forgiveness also taught me how to set boundaries. I learned that peace and wisdom must walk hand in hand. I could forgive without allowing repeated harm. I could pray for someone and still choose distance if closeness was not healthy. Forgiveness is not weakness. It is strength wrapped in grace. It is saying, "I love God more than I hate what happened to me."

Some days, forgiveness was quiet. Other days, it felt like warfare. But with each passing week, I noticed that the pain that once consumed me had begun to shrink. The memories that used to burn now reminded me of how far God had brought me. Forgiveness transformed from something I had to do into something I wanted to do, because peace felt too precious to lose.

There came a time when I realized that forgiveness was no longer just a personal healing process; it was a ministry. Every time I shared my story, someone would come up to me afterward and whisper, "I needed to hear that." Forgiveness was no longer just my private battle. It had become my testimony, proof that God truly can bring beauty from ashes.

Each time I choose forgiveness, I choose life. Each time I release the past, I make more space for the future God is writing. And each time I say, "Lord, I forgive again," heaven hears the sound of another chain breaking.

Teachable Moment: What Forgiveness Is Not

When I first began my journey of forgiveness, I thought it meant pretending nothing had happened. I thought it meant smiling politely, staying quiet, and being "the bigger person." I believed that if I truly forgave, I had to let people back into my life exactly as before. That misunderstanding caused me even more pain.

I had to learn, through tears and prayer, that forgiveness is not about pretending. It is not about denying the hurt or erasing the memory. It is not weakness, nor is it approval of what happened. True forgiveness looks very different from the passive version the world sometimes expects.

Forgiveness is not pretending you were never hurt. Many people try to move on by suppressing their pain. They say, "It's fine" or "I'm over it," even though the wound is still raw. I used to do that myself. I thought ignoring it would make it disappear. But pain that is buried alive will always resurface. Healing begins when you acknowledge what was broken and bring it into the light of God's presence. It takes courage to face the truth, but it is in truth that we find freedom.

Forgiveness is not forgetting. I often heard people say, "Just forgive and forget." But forgetting is not the goal. God did not ask me to erase my memory; He asked me to release the weight of it. The memories may remain, but they lose their power when they are no longer attached to bitterness. I can remember what happened without reliving the pain. I can look back and see lessons instead of scars.

Forgiveness is not reconciliation. This was one of the hardest lessons to learn. Reconciliation requires two willing hearts. Forgiveness, however, only requires one. You can forgive someone completely and still choose not to have a close relationship with them. That is not unforgiveness; it is wisdom. There are people you can love from a distance while still praying for their well-being. Setting healthy boundaries does not mean you are bitter; it means you have learned what peace costs and you are willing to protect it.

Forgiveness is not weakness. It takes far more strength to release anger than to hold it. Anger can make you feel powerful, but it is a false power that drains your Spirit. Forgiveness is an act of spiritual authority. It is standing before God and saying, "This hurt will not define me. This pain will not dictate who I become." Choosing peace when you could choose revenge is one of the most courageous decisions you can ever make.

Forgiveness is not instant.
It is not a switch you flip or a prayer you pray once. It is a journey, a process that unfolds layer by layer. Sometimes, you forgive one part of the situation, only for another layer of pain to surface later. That is normal. Each new layer is another opportunity for God to show you His grace. Do not rush your healing. God is patient, and He works in the deep places of the heart.

Forgiveness is not trust.
Trust is earned. Forgiveness is given. You can forgive someone and still recognize that it may take time to trust them again. Forgiveness opens the door for healing; trust builds the walls that protect it. The two are related, but they are not the same.

As I learned these truths, I began to see that forgiveness was not about others at all. It was about me and my relationship with God. Every time I forgave, I was saying, "Lord, I trust You to handle what I cannot." I stopped trying to be the judge, jury, and healer all in one. I began to understand that justice and mercy could coexist because they are both rooted in God's character.

Romans 12:19 "Do not take revenge, my dear friends, but leave room for God's wrath, for it is written: 'It is mine to avenge; I will repay,' says the Lord."

That scripture reminded me that God sees it all. Every tear, every betrayal, every sleepless night, He misses nothing. Forgiveness does not mean the person gets away with it. It means you step out of the way and let God handle it His way. His justice is always fair. His timing is always perfect.

When I finally grasped what forgiveness is not, I found clarity and peace. I stopped confusing grace with access. I realized that I could forgive sincerely while also choosing boundaries that honoured my healing. I could release someone from my heart without allowing them to re-enter my life in ways that disrupted my peace.

Forgiveness became freedom. It gave me the ability to breathe again, to love again, and to move forward without dragging the past behind me. It was no longer a burden; it became a blessing.

Every person's journey to forgiveness looks different. For some, it takes months. For others, years. What matters is not the speed, but the sincerity. When your heart truly decides to forgive, heaven begins to move on your behalf.

Forgiveness does not erase your story. It redeems it. It transforms pain into purpose and turns wounds into wisdom. The very things that once broke you become the testimony that helps others find healing, too.

Layers of Forgiveness

I discovered that forgiveness happens in layers. It is not a single act or a one-time decision. It is a journey of uncovering wounds that run deeper than you first imagined. The first layer is the surface choice, the decision to forgive. But once you make that choice, God begins to reveal the hidden places where pain has been stored.

There were layers I did not even know existed until I started peeling them back. The first was forgiving the obvious, the betrayal, the lies, the broken promises. Those were the wounds I could name easily. But as time went on, I began to uncover other layers that were more subtle yet equally painful. I had to forgive the silence, the absence, and the emotional distance that left me feeling unseen and unheard. I had to forgive the moments when I begged to be understood, only to be met with indifference. I had to forgive not only what was done to me but what was withheld from me.

Each time I faced another layer, I felt the old ache rise again. Sometimes I wondered if I would ever be free. Forgiving once felt hard enough; why did it seem like I had to do it again and again? I came to realize that each layer represented a different depth of healing. Forgiveness is like tending a garden. You pull one weed, and beneath it lies another root buried deeper. The goal is not just to make the surface look good. It is to remove what grows beneath so that new life can take hold.

This process was exhausting at times. There were days I wanted to stop peeling back layers because each one brought fresh tears. But I also noticed something beautiful happening. Every time I surrendered another layer, I felt lighter. Every time I revisited the pain and handed it to God, I made more room for His peace to dwell in me. Forgiveness was no longer just about freeing someone else. It was about allowing God to set me free.

One of the most difficult layers was forgiving the version of myself who stayed too long. I had to forgive the woman who ignored the red flags, who tried to fix everything alone, who thought love meant enduring more than was healthy. That was the hardest layer of all because it required self-compassion. I realized I had been holding myself hostage to guilt and regret, as if punishing myself could somehow rewrite the past.

God met me in that place of self-blame with quiet tenderness. Through tears, I heard His whisper, "You did the best you could with what you knew then." Those words washed over me like healing rain. I began to see myself not as a failure, but as a survivor of a season that was meant to teach me endurance and faith.

Each layer of forgiveness became an act of worship. I learned that every time I released something painful, I was making space for something sacred. Forgiveness stripped me of bitterness and clothed me in peace. It removed heaviness and replaced it with hope.

One morning during prayer, I felt led to write down everyone, every situation, and every emotion I still needed to forgive. It was a long list, some names, some memories, and even some dreams that never came true. I laid the list on my Bible and prayed, "Lord, this is too much for me to carry, but nothing is too much for You." As I prayed, a sense of Release filled the room. It was as if God Himself was lifting the weight off my shoulders, layer by layer.

That experience taught me that forgiveness is not about time. It is about willingness. You do not have to rush the process, but you do have to stay open. Some layers will take weeks, others years. Each time you are ready, God will gently lead you to the next one. He never forces healing. He invites it.

Forgiveness also revealed unexpected blessings. As the layers fell away, I noticed my laughter returning, my creativity awakening, and my heart softening toward others. I began to see people not as threats, but as souls who, like me, were walking their own roads of brokenness and grace. The empathy that grew in me became one of the most beautiful fruits of forgiveness.

Luke 6:37 says, "Forgive, and you will be forgiven." I used to read that verse as a command, but now I see it as a promise. Forgiveness opens a flow of grace. As I extend grace, more grace flows back into my life. The more I released, the more God filled me with peace, purpose, and understanding.

Looking back, I understand now that forgiveness in layers is not a sign of weakness or incomplete healing. It is a sign that God is working intensely, removing what does not belong and planting something more substantial in its place. Every layer I surrendered brought me closer to freedom. Every tear I cried watered the seeds of new life that were taking root in my heart.

Forgiveness is not a straight road; it is a spiral upward. You may revisit the same place, but each time, you rise higher. You become lighter. You grow wiser. You see clearly.

Today, I can say that every layer I peeled back was worth it. What once felt like breaking was actually rebuilding. What once felt like loss became the foundation for new strength. And what once felt like the end was only the beginning of God's beautiful restoration.

A Story of Release

I remember a particular Sunday when the weight of bitterness felt unbearable. I had gone to church out of routine, but my heart was heavy. During worship, the lyrics spoke about God's mercy being new every morning. I felt a gentle nudge in my Spirit: *"As I have given you mercy, extend mercy to him."*

I wanted to resist, but tears streamed down my face. I realized forgiveness was not just about him. It was about me being free to worship without chains. That day, I whispered again, "I forgive." I left the service lighter, not because the pain was erased, but because I was no longer carrying it alone.

A.R.E. Focus: Release Resentment

When I created the A.R.E. framework, Acknowledge, Release, Empower- it was born from my own process of healing. I realized that forgiveness was not just a moment of saying, "I forgive." It was a posture of the heart that had to be practiced daily. The second step, *Release*, became the bridge between pain and peace.

Resentment is heavy. It clings to the soul like chains, keeping you bound to the very thing you want freedom from. At first, resentment can feel justified. It makes you believe you are protecting yourself. But over time, it poisons everything it touches: your joy, your faith, your relationships, and even your health. The Bible says in **Hebrews 12:15, "See to it that no bitter root grows up to cause trouble and defile many."**

Bitterness does not stay contained. It spreads. And the longer it lives in your heart, the harder it becomes to see clearly. Releasing resentment, therefore, is not a favour you do for someone else. It is a necessity for your own healing.

I had to learn this the hard way. There were days when I told myself I had forgiven, yet one thought, one memory, or one conversation could stir everything back up again. I realized I had released words, but not emotions. My lips said, "I forgive," but my heart still carried the weight. That was when I began to ask God to teach me how to release truly.

Releasing resentment does not happen by pretending you are fine. It happens through intentional surrender. Every time bitterness rises, you hand it back to God and say, "Lord, I do not want to carry this anymore." That simple act—though it may need to be repeated often—creates space for peace to enter.

Step 1: Identify What You Are Still Holding

Start by asking yourself, "What do I still feel when I think about what happened?" Please write it down. Do not filter or judge your feelings. Let the truth flow honestly. You might discover anger, disappointment, betrayal, or sadness that you did not even realize was still there.

Awareness is the first step toward Release. You cannot let go of what you have not acknowledged.

Step 2: Name the Cost of Holding On

Ask yourself, "What is resentment costing me?" It might be your peace of mind, your sleep, your ability to trust, or your joy. When I saw how resentment was stealing my energy and keeping me stuck, I realized it was simply not worth it. The price was too high.

Sometimes we think holding on gives us power, but in reality, it keeps us powerless. It keeps us living in the past while God is trying to lead us into the future.

Step 3: Replace Resentment with Renewal

Releasing resentment is not just about letting go of something negative; it is about replacing it with something life-giving. Every time you catch yourself replaying the hurt, stop and speak a word of renewal instead. Say a prayer. Speak a scripture. Declare truth.

For me, I often returned to ***Ephesians 4:31 -32: "Get rid of all bitterness, rage, and anger… Be kind and compassionate to one another, forgiving each other, just as in Christ God forgave you."***

I wrote those words on sticky notes and placed them around my home on my mirror, refrigerator, and even my car dashboard. They became daily reminders that I had the power to choose peace over poison.

Step 4: Practice Emotional Release

Sometimes, release happens through tears. Sometimes through writing. Sometimes through prayer. I found journaling to be one of the most powerful tools. When I poured my emotions onto the page, I could see the heaviness I had been carrying. And when I finished writing, I would close my journal and say, "Lord, I release this to You." It was symbolic, but it was also sacred.

There were nights I cried until I fell asleep mid-prayer. I learned that God does not need fancy words. He needs an honest heart. Every tear you cry is a language heaven understands.

Step 5: Choose to Release Again Tomorrow

Release is not a one-time event. It is a rhythm. There will be days when you feel light and peaceful, and days when the pain returns. On those hard days, remind yourself that healing is not linear. Each time you release again, the hold of resentment weakens.

A Practical Tool: The Release Box

Find a small box or container and label it *The Release Box*. Whenever a painful thought or memory arises, write it on a slip of paper. Be specific. Then pray over it and place it in the box. Once a month, take a moment to revisit the box, pray again, and physically discard the papers, perhaps by shredding or burning them safely.

It may sound simple, but it is deeply symbolic. Each act of letting go reminds your Spirit that you are choosing freedom.

A.R.E. Reflection

- **Acknowledge:** Be honest about the emotions you still carry.

- **Release:** Surrender those emotions to God's care.

- **Empower:** Allow the peace of God to fill the space that pain once occupied.

Every time you release resentment, you make room for empowerment. You make space for joy to return, for laughter to find its way back into your days, and for faith to breathe again.

Daily Affirmation

"I am releasing the weight of resentment and walking freely in the peace of God. I am no longer chained to the past. My heart is open, my Spirit is light, and my future is free."

Releasing resentment is not weakness: it is worship. It is saying, "God, I trust You more than my emotions. I believe Your plan for my peace is better than my plan for revenge." When you live in that truth, you walk not only in healing but in victory.

Practical Tool: The Forgiveness Letter

Take time to write a letter to the person who hurt you. Pour out every hurt, every disappointment, every betrayal onto the page. Do not hold back. Write down the things you never said, the tears you never shed publicly, the words you swallowed.

Then, at the end of the letter, write your decision to forgive. Write words like, "I choose to forgive you, not because you asked or because you deserve it, but because I deserve peace."

You never have to send the letter. The freedom comes not from their reaction, but from the act of releasing what you have carried for too long. Some people burn the letter as a symbol of letting go. Others keep it as a testimony of their journey. The choice is yours.

Reflection Exercise

- Who do I still hold in my heart with unforgiveness?

- What lies have I told myself about why I cannot forgive?

- How might forgiveness free me more than it frees them?

Take time to write out your answers. Often, seeing your thoughts on paper reveals truths you did not realize were hidden in your heart.

Daily Affirmations

Speak these affirmations over yourself each day until they become part of your belief:

1. I release resentment and choose peace.

2. Forgiving does not make me weak; it makes me free.

3. God's mercy toward me empowers me to extend mercy to others.

4. My healing is not dependent on another person's apology.

5. Forgiveness is my pathway to freedom.

The Fruit of Forgiveness

As I continued to practice forgiveness, something beautiful began to happen. My heart started to soften in ways I did not expect. I noticed it first in small moments. I no longer bristled when his name was mentioned. I could see him without feeling that familiar rush of anger or that tightening in my chest. The bitterness that once clouded every thought began to lift. Over time, I even found myself praying for his well-being, not out of duty or religious habit, but from a sincere desire that he experience healing too.

This was not something I could have manufactured

on my own. It was not the result of positive thinking or willpower. It was the fruit of God's Spirit quietly working in me. *Galatians 5:22–23 describes the fruit of the Spirit as love, joy, peace, patience, kindness, goodness, faithfulness, gentleness, and self-control.* Forgiveness made room for those qualities to flourish in my heart.

Each time I chose forgiveness over resentment, I felt love take root where hatred once lived. Each time I released an offence, peace replaced anxiety. Each time I prayed for someone who had hurt me, joy returned to my Spirit. It was as if forgiveness had cleared the soil of my heart, allowing God's fruit to grow in fresh, fertile ground.

The Transformation Within

Before forgiveness took root, I had become guarded, even with those who loved me. I did not realize how much pain had hardened me. I smiled on the outside but built invisible walls around my heart to keep anyone from getting too close. I told myself I was protecting my peace, but I was really protecting my pain.

As God continued to heal me, those walls began to crumble. I found myself laughing again, connecting with people without fear of being hurt, and trusting that not everyone would break what I had worked so hard to rebuild. Forgiveness did not erase my memories, but it transformed the meaning behind them. Where I once saw only pain, I began to see purpose.

The deeper I forgave, the freer I became. Freedom did not arrive in one grand moment. It came quietly, like dawn after a long night. I began to feel lighter, not because my past had changed, but because its power over me had faded.

Teachable Moment: Forgiveness and Boundaries

Forgiveness does not mean allowing yourself to be mistreated again. You can forgive and still say no. You can release resentment and still protect your peace. Forgiveness is about letting go of bitterness, not about tolerating abuse. In fact, setting boundaries is part of living in the freedom that forgiveness brings.

Boundaries are an expression of self-respect and wisdom. They communicate that while you wish the other person well, you are no longer willing to live in dysfunction. Jesus Himself modelled boundaries. He loved everyone, but He did not entrust himself to everyone. There were moments when He withdrew to pray, moments when He walked away from crowds, and moments when He allowed distance for the sake of peace.

Healthy boundaries honour both God and yourself. They create space where peace can grow. They say, "I forgive you, but I am not returning to the chaos." They remind you that grace and wisdom must walk hand in hand.

Living in Grace

Looking back now, I realize that forgiveness was never about erasing the past. It was about embracing the present and reframing the story. The hurt happened. The betrayal was real. But forgiveness allowed me to view my journey through the lens of grace rather than bitterness.

I began to see how God had used even the most painful parts to shape me. The betrayal that once broke me became the soil where my purpose began to bloom. The tears that I once felt wasted became the water that nourished my growth. I saw how God was weaving the threads of my story into something meaningful.

Romans 8:28 "And we know that in all things God works for the good of those who love Him." Even the heartbreak. Even the silence. Even the disappointment. None of it was wasted.

A New Perspective

As my heart healed, I began to look back with gratitude instead of grief. What once felt like the end of my story had become the beginning of my testimony. My scars were no longer signs of defeat; they were proof of survival. They reminded me that God can turn what was meant for harm into good.

I started to see forgiveness as a form of spiritual transformation. It was no longer about the other person. It was about my relationship with God and the woman I was becoming. I was not the same person who had entered the storm. I had learned to love deeper, to discern better, and to walk lighter. Forgiveness did not make me weak. It made me wise. It made me whole.

When I think of the fruit of forgiveness now, I see a woman who can smile without pretending. I see someone who can remember the past without reliving it. I see joy that is not dependent on circumstances and peace that no one can take away.

A Reflection for You

Take a moment to reflect on your own journey. Who or what still holds space in your heart through resentment or regret? What fruit might be waiting to grow once you release it? Ask God to help you loosen your grip. As you do, you will find that the same Spirit that worked in me is ready to work in you.

Forgiveness will not always feel easy, but it will always be worth it. The more you forgive, the more you reflect God's heart. The more you release, the freer you become. And one day, you will look back, just as I did, and realize that what once felt like breaking was actually the moment your soul began to bloom.

Prayer

Father, You have forgiven me more than I could ever repay. Help me release the grip of resentment and walk in the freedom of forgiveness. Heal my heart and teach me to see others through Your mercy. When bitterness rises, remind me that Your grace is stronger. I place those who have hurt me into Your hands and choose peace for myself. Amen.

Closing Thought

Climbing the mountain of forgiveness is a challenging task. It is steep, rocky, and often painful. There will be moments when you want to turn back, moments when the climb feels impossible. But with every step, the load grows lighter.

When you reach the top, you realize forgiveness was never about letting someone else go free: it was about letting yourself breathe again. It was about reclaiming your peace, your joy, and your future. Forgiveness is not the end of your story. It is the beginning of your freedom.

6.

REBUILDING THE BRIDGES

After forgiveness came something I never expected: the slow rebuilding of relationships that I thought were forever destroyed. My ex-husband and I had to learn how to communicate again, not as husband and wife, but as parents of the children we both loved deeply.

At first, conversations were awkward and tense. We often tiptoed around sensitive topics, careful not to ignite arguments that lingered beneath the surface. Sometimes silence felt safer than speaking. I would leave those moments frustrated, wondering if peace was even possible.

But as the bitterness in my heart lifted, I began to notice a change. Forgiveness softened me. My words carried less sharpness. My tone shifted. I was no longer fighting to win; I was learning to seek peace. And in that shift, a new foundation began to emerge.

Learning a New Way to Communicate

Rebuilding any relationship after deep hurt requires patience. It is not about pretending nothing happened or forcing closeness where trust is still fragile. It is about choosing a different posture. I began to listen more and speak less. When disagreements arose, I prayed before responding. I asked God to help me see the person, not just the pain.

At times, I failed. There were days when old wounds

resurfaced, and my words carried more emotion than grace. But even then, I could feel God nudging me to pause, to breathe, to try again. The Holy Spirit became my teacher in communication. Every time I chose calm instead of criticism, I was laying a plank on a broken bridge.

Little by little, the atmosphere changed. A simple exchange about our children's school schedules no longer felt like walking through a minefield. There were moments of shared laughter, small reminders that peace was possible. We were not the same people we had been, but we were learning how to respect one another in this new chapter of our lives.

Peace for the Sake of the Children

The most beautiful outcome of this new approach was the peace it brought to our children. They no longer had to brace themselves for tension when both parents were in the same room. They could breathe easier, knowing that the love for them was stronger than the hurt between us.

One day, at a school event, our son looked up at both of us and smiled. It was a genuine, relieved smile, the kind that said, "Everything will be okay." That moment melted years of bitterness. It reminded me why forgiveness was worth it. Reconciliation, even partial, can bring healing to everyone connected to the story.

Children notice the tone of a conversation, the tension in a room, and the softness or hardness of a parent's voice. When we choose peace, we give them a model of strength that is rooted in grace, not anger. I wanted my children to see that broken relationships can still produce healthy interactions. They could see that forgiveness was not weakness; it was maturity, wisdom, and faith in action.

Boundaries and Balance

Rebuilding bridges does not mean returning to the same kind of relationship you once had. It does not erase the need for boundaries. Forgiveness opens the door to peace, but boundaries keep that peace safe. I learned that it was okay to limit certain conversatispecific walk away when old arguments resurfaced, and to choose kindness without allowing disrespect.

Boundaries are not walls; they are guardrails. They protect what God has healed. I could be respectful and cooperative without reopening wounds that no longer needed to be touched. This understanding helped me let go of guilt about what reconciliation should look like. It was not about friendship or constant closeness; it was about mutual respect and emotional stability.

Living in Peace

This was not about becoming best friends or pretending the past never happened. It was about recognizing that brokenness did not have to define our future interactions. Rebuilding bridges is not about erasing cracks; it is about strengthening them. It is about choosing to build a new path across them.

Romans 12:18 became my compass: ***"If it is possible, as far as it depends on you, live at peace with everyone."***

That scripture reminded me that peace does not always depend on the other person. It depends on the posture of my own heart. I could not control his responses. I could not change his choices. But I could choose my attitude, my words, and my boundaries.

The day I finally embraced that truth, something shifted inside me. I realized that peace was not something someone else could give or take away from me. It was a gift from God that I could protect, nurture, and walk in, regardless of what others did. I stopped waiting for apologies that might never come. I stopped expecting understanding from someone who could not see my heart. Instead, I started focusing on what I could give—respect, patience, and calm communication.

Little by little, we began to rebuild. A simple exchange of information about the children without hostility. A shared smile at a school event when our son performed on stage. A respectful conversation about a decision that affected our daughter. These may sound small, but for us, they were monumental. Each plank laid across the broken bridge felt like a step forward.

I remember one particular day at our daughter's graduation. We were both seated in the audience, and for the first time in years, there was no tension in the air. We both cheered for her, both proud and emotional, and when our eyes met briefly, there was a quiet acknowledgment between us. We were no longer enemies. We were parents united by love for our children and guided by the grace of forgiveness. That moment was not about friendship or reconciliation; it was about peace. It was about showing our children that maturity means choosing grace over grudges.

The most powerful moment came when my children saw us together without conflict clouding the room. They no longer had to brace themselves for awkward silences or quick exits. They could relax and just be present. That alone was a miracle. It showed them that respect and forgiveness can create healing spaces, even when relationships remain changed.

Peace, I learned, is not the absence of pain or disagreement. It is the presence of understanding. It is the quiet strength that allows you to stand firm in love even when the past could easily pull you into bitterness. It is choosing not to reopen old wounds simply because you know you could. It is responding with calm where you once reacted in anger.

A Teachable Moment: The Strength of Quiet Grace

One of the most powerful lessons I learned during this time was that reconciliation does not require loud gestures. It grows quietly through consistent choices. There were no grand apologies, no dramatic scenes of reunion. Instead, there were small moments of grace, like choosing to respond kindly when frustration tried to rise, or saying a silent prayer before picking up the phone.

"If it is possible, as far as it depends on you, live at peace with everyone." I could not control anyone else's actions, but I could control mine. I could be the one who planted peace, even if it was not always reciprocated. I learned that reconciliation is not always about restoring a relationship to what it once was. Sometimes it is simply about learning to stand in the same space without hostility, to coexist without carrying resentment.

The Fruit of Peace

As months went by, peace began to settle in like a gentle dawn. It did not erase the past, but it made the present bearable and even hopeful. The more I focused on peace, the more I saw God's fingerprints on the process. Forgiveness had created room for grace, and grace had paved the way for understanding.

This experience also deepened my compassion for others. I started to see that many people carry silent pain from broken relationships. Some are trying to rebuild, others are still trapped in anger. I began to encourage others with my own story, reminding them that peace is possible when we allow God to lead. Even if reconciliation is not perfect, even if trust is slow to grow, peace is still a victory.

.

The Strength in Stillness

There is power in stillness. It takes strength to pause instead of reacting, to listen instead of defending, to pray instead of arguing. Every time I chose silence over sarcasm, grace over gossip, I felt myself growing stronger. I began to see that peace is not passive. It is an active stance, one that takes courage and discipline.

When you choose peace, you are not surrendering to weakness. You are rising in strength. It takes far more maturity to respond with wisdom than to retaliate with words. Each peaceful interaction became a small victory, proof that forgiveness had truly taken root in my heart.

I often think of **Philippians 4:7,** which says, **"And the peace of God, which surpasses all understanding, will guard your hearts and your minds in Christ Jesus."** That verse describes exactly what I experienced. God's peace became my guard. It protected me from slipping back into bitterness. It reminded me that I did not need to win an argument to feel secure. My peace was already anchored in Him.

Teaching Peace by Example

Living in peace also transformed how I approached life beyond that relationship. It changed how I treated others, how I led in ministry, and how I interacted with my children. They began to notice the difference, too. One day, my daughter said, "Mom, you don't get angry the same way anymore." He was right. I had learned that peace is not pretending to be calm; it is choosing to stay anchored when everything around you tempts you to drift.

Through my example, my children learned that forgiveness is not weakness. It is strength under control. It is being able to face what once broke you without letting it break you again. They saw that you can release someone from your heart and still honour God in your actions. That realization became one of the greatest legacies I could give them.

The Weight of Example

What surprised me most in rebuilding was how much it affected my children. They were no longer children in the literal sense, but our relationship still carried weight with them. When they saw us speak respectfully, they learned that even fractured relationships can be navigated with civility. When they saw us put aside bitterness for their sake, they learned that love is stronger than conflict.

One of my sons later said to me, "Mom, seeing you and Dad talk without fighting gave me hope that not everything ends badly." His words pierced me in the best way. I realized our healing was not just about us. It was shaping the next generation.

A Story of Practice

There was one afternoon when I needed to ask my ex-husband about a financial matter concerning our children. I rehearsed the conversation in my head for hours, afraid it would spiral into accusations. When we finally spoke, I braced myself. But to my surprise, it was calm. We disagreed on details, but we listened to each other. I chose not to escalate, and he mirrored that choice. The conversation ended on a clear note, not in conflict.

That evening, I journaled about it. For the first time, I realized I had put into practice what Romans 12:18 had taught me. I had chosen peace over pride. It was a small win, but small wins matter. They add up to stronger bridges.

A.R.E. Focus: Empower Relationships

- **Acknowledge:** Admit where the fractures are real. Do not minimize the pain or pretend it never happened. Naming the wound gives space for healing.

- **Release:** Let go of the need to control how others respond. You cannot force reconciliation. You can only bring your best self.

- **Empower:** Choose small steps that build peace, even if reconciliation is not complete. A kind word, a prayer, or a respectful silence can carry more weight than you imagine.

Practical Tool: Bridge Mapping

Take time to reflect on one fractured relationship in your life. Draw a simple bridge on a page. On one side, write your name. On the other side, write the other person's name.

In the middle, write small steps you could take to bring peace. These might include:

- Offering a kind word.

- Praying for them daily.

- Choosing forgiveness again when old memories surface.

- Setting a boundary that creates safety and clarity.

- Refraining from speaking negatively about them to others.

Writing these steps creates a visual reminder that building bridges is a process. It is one plank at a time, not the whole structure in a day.

Reflection Exercise

Take a moment to reflect on your own relationships. Are there bridges that need rebuilding? Are there words you could speak with more grace, or moments where silence might speak louder than defence? Living in peace begins with acknowledging where you can bring calm instead of chaos.

Ask yourself:

- What does peace look like for me in this season?

- Is there someone I need to forgive, or someone I need to communicate with differently?

- How can I protect my peace without closing my heart?

Write your thoughts down and pray over them. Invite God into the process. His Spirit will guide you in what to say, when to stay silent, and how to carry peace even into difficult conversations.

Daily Affirmations

1. I am a peacemaker, and I choose words that bring life.

2. I can forgive and still create healthy boundaries.

3. With God's help, I am rebuilding bridges toward peace.

4. My healing is not dependent on another person's choices.

5. Every act of respect is a seed of restoration.

The Power of Respect

Respect became the language that made rebuilding possible. It was not a single choice but a daily decision. I did not always agree with him, but I could still choose to speak with respect. Respect is not weakness. It is strength under control. It is not about pretending the past never happened, but about creating a foundation for peace in the present. It does not erase history, but it paves the way for future interactions to happen without hostility.

When I looked at him only through the lens of hurt, all I could see was betrayal. Every memory reminded me of disappointment. Every word he spoke seemed to carry echoes of old pain. But when I chose to see him through the lens of respect, I began to view him differently. I began to see him as a flawed human being, just like me, capable of both good and failure. That shift opened the door for civility.

Respect was not something he had to earn all over again. I chose to extend it because of who I was becoming. I realized that respect had nothing to do with him. It was about me. It was about honouring God in my words and actions. It was about living in a way that reflected the healing I had prayed for.

The Quiet Work of Honour

Philippians 2:3–4 reminds us: "Do nothing out of selfish ambition or vain conceit. Rather, in humility value others above yourselves, not looking to your own interests but each of you to the interests of the others." Respect flows out of humility, not pride. It requires you to see the other person as valuable, even when they have hurt you.

At first, this verse challenged me. I thought, How can I value someone who broke my heart? How can I show kindness when I am still healing? Yet over time, I learned that humility is not about exalting someone else at your expense. It is about trusting God to handle what is beyond your control. When I practiced humility, I stopped trying to prove my point or defend my pain. I began to speak from a place of calm rather than chaos.

Respect became my peacekeeper. When tension threatened to rise, I would take a deep breath and silently pray, "Lord, let my words be seasoned with grace." Sometimes I needed to pause before speaking, to make sure I was responding in love rather than reacting in hurt. Other times, I chose silence because peace mattered more than being right.

Respect as a Reflection of Healing

I learned that true healing changes the way you communicate. Before forgiveness, every conversation felt like a battle. After healing, it became an opportunity to demonstrate growth. I no longer needed to win arguments or prove my worth. I no longer felt the need to remind him of everything he had done wrong. That was freedom.

There were moments when he would test my patience, intentionally or not. Old habits have a way of resurfacing. But instead of reacting as I once would have, I began to view those moments as chances to practice restraint. Each time I responded with respect instead of resentment, I felt God's presence strengthen me.

Proverbs 15:1 says, "A gentle answer turns away wrath, but a harsh word stirs up anger." I had seen this truth play out countless times. Gentleness disarmed tension. A calm voice brought clarity where arguments once brought confusion. Respect was not about agreement; it was about grace.

Teaching by Example

Something unexpected happened as I walked in respect. My children began to notice. They saw the change in me. They heard the way I spoke and watched how I carried myself. Without realizing it, I was teaching them what mature love and forgiveness looked like. They saw that respect was possible even when relationships shift or end.

One afternoon, my daughter said, "Mom, I'm proud of how you talk to Dad." Her words touched me deeply because I knew she had seen the worst of our pain. She had witnessed the anger, the silence, and the distance. Now she was seeing the fruit of healing. That was the most remarkable testimony I could ever give her.

Respect had turned what could have been bitterness into a living lesson of grace. It showed my children that forgiveness does not erase accountability, but it does make reconciliation possible. They learned that you can disagree and still be dignified. They learned that love does not have to vanish when relationships change; it can evolve into something wiser and kinder.

Respecting Myself

Learning to respect him also helped me learn to respect myself. I realized that respect was not about lowering my standards or ignoring boundaries. It was about maintaining my integrity. Speaking respectfully meant I was in control of my emotions, not having my emotions control me.

Respect is a two-way gift. When you give it to others, you strengthen it in yourself. It reinforces your sense of dignity and self-worth. You realize you do not have to become bitter to be strong. You can be kind without being naive. You can be firm without being harsh.

I learned that respecting myself also meant walking away from conversations that went nowhere, refusing to dwell in the past, and prioritizing peace over pride. It meant forgiving without returning to toxicity. It meant recognizing that while I could not change others, I could change how I responded to them.

A Heart at Rest

Over time, respect became more than a principle. It became a rhythm. It changed the way I interacted not only with my ex-husband but with everyone around me. It reminded me that I could live peacefully without needing validation.

Respect, when rooted in faith, brings rest. It quiets the inner battles that once consumed your mind. It allows you to move through life with grace and confidence, knowing that your strength comes from God and not from controlling others.

Every time I chose respect, I chose peace. Every time I spoke gently, I planted a seed of healing. And as those seeds took root, I saw the fruit of restoration, not in the relationship as it once was, but in the woman I was becoming.

Reconciliation vs. Restoration

It is essential to distinguish between reconciliation and restoration. Reconciliation means re-establishing a relationship. Restoration refers to the process of returning something to its original state. Not all relationships will be restored to what they were, but some can be reconciled enough to function in peace.

God does not always restore things to their previous form. Sometimes, he builds something new from the ashes. ***Isaiah 61:3 reminds us that He gives beauty for ashes.*** That means what is rebuilt may look different, but it can still be beautiful.

Beyond My Story

Rebuilding bridges is not limited to ex-spouses. It applies to friendships that ended in harsh words, family ties severed by misunderstandings, or even workplace relationships scarred by conflict. The principles remain the same: forgiveness first, boundaries second, peace as the ultimate goal.

I once spoke with a woman who had not spoken to her sister in years. Their argument had started over something small but had grown into a silence that stretched across decades. She told me she finally decided to send her sister a card with three simple words: "I forgive you." That card opened the door for conversations that had seemed impossible. Their relationship was never the same as before, but they built a bridge of civility and care.

The Gift of Peace

Peace became the greatest gift of rebuilding. Not the absence of conflict, but the presence of calm. Not pretending, but choosing. Not perfection, but progress.

Every time I chose respect, I chose peace. Every time I chose to release control, I chose peace. Every time I set a healthy boundary, I choose peace. And that peace spilled over into every area of my life.

Jesus said in ***Matthew 5:9, "Blessed are the peacemakers, for they will be called children of God."*** Building bridges has made me a peacemaker, not just within my own family, but also as a witness to others. People saw that healing was possible. People saw that peace could rise from the rubble.

Prayer

Lord, teach me to be a peacemaker. Please show me where to build bridges and where to set healthy boundaries. Help me walk in wisdom, love, and grace as I interact with others. Remind me that peace begins in my own heart. May every word I speak and every step I take reflect Your mercy and compassion. Amen.

Closing Thought

Rebuilding bridges is not about returning to what was;

it's about building something new. It is about creating something new, something more substantial, something rooted in peace rather than bitterness. You may not walk every bridge to its far side, but even laying down a single plank is an act of courage. It is a step toward healing, freedom, and the kind of peace that Romans 12:18 promises is possible.

The cracks in your past do not disqualify you. They remind you of what has been endured. With forgiveness as the foundation, respect as the framework, and peace as the goal, even the most fractured relationships can find a path toward redemption.

7.

STEPPING INTO A NEW CHAPTER

The day came when I realized my divorce no longer defined me. The pain was part of my story, but it was not my entire story. I had walked through nights of tears, moments of doubt, and days when I felt invisible. Yet gradually, I began to see that the storm had not destroyed me. It had refined me. A new chapter had begun.

For years, my identity had been tied to being someone's wife, someone's support system, someone's partner in a shared life. When that ended, I felt stripped of all the roles I once knew. But what I did not realize at first was that God was inviting me to rediscover the woman I had always been beneath those titles. I was still His daughter. I was still chosen. I was still called.

Healing had slowly rebuilt me, piece by piece. Forgiveness had unlocked chains I did not know I carried. Now I stood stronger, more grounded, and more aware of who I truly was. The woman who once cried herself to sleep was now laughing again. The one who once questioned her worth was learning to see herself through the eyes of grace.

I felt free in this chapter. Free to rediscover my passions. Free to travel without hesitation. Free to laugh without guilt and to dream new dreams without apology. Freedom meant embracing my identity, not as a wife or a title, but as a woman created in God's image: a woman with purpose, with power, and with an assignment that no one could take away.

Rediscovering Joy

At first, I did not know what to do with that freedom. It felt strange to make decisions without consulting anyone else. I had spent so many years considering another person's preferences that I had forgotten how to listen to my own heart. I began by doing small things that brought me joy. I took long walks by the water, something that had always calmed my spirit. I travelled more, even if it meant going alone. I explored new places and rediscovered the beauty of solitude.

There was a sweetness in waking up to quiet mornings, sipping tea by the window, and watching the sunrise without rushing anywhere. I started journaling again, not about pain this time, but about hope. My entries were filled with prayers of gratitude and dreams of what could be. Slowly, I began to see that this season was not punishment. It was preparation.

Psalm 30:11 "You turned my mourning into dancing; you removed my sackcloth and clothed me with joy." That scripture described exactly what God was doing in my life. He was turning what had once been ashes into something beautiful.

Learning to Love Again

Yes, I fell in love again, but that is another story for another time. Love after loss is complicated. It comes with both joy and caution. The heart that has been broken learns to love differently. It becomes wiser, more intentional, and more prayerful.

When love found me again, I was no longer the same

woman I once was. I was not searching for someone to complete me or to fix what was broken. I had learned that only God could do that. Instead, I was looking for companionship rooted in purpose and mutual respect.

Relationships after divorce require wisdom, discernment, and prayer. It is easy to rush into something new to fill the void that loss leaves behind, but true healing cannot be rushed. Love must come from a place of wholeness, not desperation. If you decide to start another relationship, be sure of what you are getting into. Take time to heal first. Invite God into every decision. Let Him guide your heart and your steps.

Proverbs 3:5–6 was another scripture that anchored me during that time: ***"Trust in the Lord with all your heart and lean not on your own understanding; in all your ways acknowledge Him, and He will make your paths straight."*** Every time I felt uncertain or afraid, I would return to that verse. It reminded me that I did not have to navigate love or life alone. God was still directing my story.

Purpose Reborn

As I embraced this new chapter, I discovered that freedom also meant responsibility. God had given me another chance, not only to live but to live well. I started serving again, using my story to encourage women who were walking through similar pain. I realized that my healing was not only for me; it was meant to help others find theirs.

I began writing and speaking about forgiveness, about resilience, about finding peace in the middle of heartbreak. Each time I shared, I could see the tears and nods of recognition from women who felt unseen. My story reminded them that it was possible to rise again. It was possible to build a life of meaning after brokenness.

Ephesians 2:10 says, "For we are His workmanship, created in Christ Jesus for good works, which God prepared beforehand that we should walk in them." I began walking in those good works with renewed purpose. What once felt like the end of everything had become the beginning of my calling.

Freedom as Worship

There was something sacred about freedom that I had never known before. It was not wild or reckless. It was peaceful and rooted. It was knowing that I could stand alone and still be whole. It was worshiping God not because everything was perfect, but because He had carried me through what had once seemed impossible.

Worship became more than songs on Sunday. It became my lifestyle. Every sunrise felt like a promise. Every smile was a testimony. Every moment of peace was proof that God's grace runs deeper than any wound. I had thought freedom meant doing whatever I wanted. But now I knew true freedom was found in surrender: trusting that God's plan for me was better than anything I could design for myself.

A Heart Restored

Looking back, I see that healing did not erase my scars. It transformed them into reminders of God's faithfulness. I can talk about my past without pain because I see the purpose in it. I can love again because I know what love is not. I can stand alone because I have learned that I am never truly alone.

The woman I am today is not the same woman who

walked through that storm. She is stronger, wiser, and more rooted in grace. She knows that life after heartbreak is not just possible: it can be beautiful.

The day I realized my divorce no longer defined me was the day I finally understood that my identity was not tied to any relationship but to the One who never leaves. I had been shattered, but I was still standing. And in standing, I found freedom.

A New Anthem

Isaiah 43:19 became my anthem:
"See, I am doing a new thing! Now it springs up; do you not perceive it? I am making a way in the wilderness and streams in the wasteland."

Those words felt alive, almost as if God Himself was speaking directly into my spirit. Every time I read them, I felt a stirring of hope that something beautiful was beginning to grow, even in places that had once felt barren.

God was showing me that my story was not ending in brokenness. It was blossoming into something new. Forgiveness had cleared the ground. Healing had prepared the soil. And now it was time to plant seeds of joy, purpose, and legacy.

For so long, I had been focused on survival. Every prayer had been about getting through one more day, one more trial, one more wave of emotion. But now, something had shifted. I was no longer praying to survive. I was praying to thrive. I wanted to see what God could do with a heart that had been shattered and restored. I wanted to walk into the "new thing" He had promised.

The wilderness had once felt endless, but I began to realize that even deserts bloom when God sends His rain. Every lesson learned, every tear shed, had been watering the soil of my future. What once looked like a wasteland of regret was becoming fertile ground for growth.

God was doing something beneath the surface, even when I could not see it. Healing had not been quick or easy, but it had been thorough, and each moment of surrender had softened the hardened parts of my heart. Each act of forgiveness had pulled up weeds of bitterness that once choked my peace. Each prayer whispered through tears had been a seed planted in faith.

When I looked back, I saw that God had been faithful at every stage. He had never left me, even in my darkest nights. He had walked with me through grief and guided me through uncertainty. Now, he was calling me to lift my eyes from the past and look toward the horizon. It was time to walk in the newness He had prepared.

That verse from Isaiah became more than words on a page. It became a declaration over my life. It became a song in my spirit. When I felt afraid to take a new step, I would whisper, "God is doing a new thing." When doubts crept in, I reminded myself, "He is making a way in the wilderness." When I felt unworthy of joy, I would remember, "He is bringing streams into dry places."

This anthem carried me through the transition from healing to purpose. It reminded me that God specializes in resurrection stories. What He restores, He multiplies. What He heals, He repurposes. I began to dream again. Not small, cautious dreams, but bold, faith-filled ones. I started envisioning how my life could reflect His glory, how my story could inspire others who were still in the storm.

That new thing God was doing did not happen all at once. It unfolded in divine timing. A new project here, a new connection there, a renewed sense of confidence rising quietly in my heart. I began to see that walking in purpose was not about perfection. It was about obedience. Each day, I chose to believe that God was still writing my story, even when I could not see the next chapter.

As I stepped into this new season, I carried the lessons of the past but no longer their weight. I had been refined by fire, not consumed by it. I had been shaped by sorrow, but not defined by it. My anthem was clear: God was doing a new thing, and I was ready to perceive it.

Every sunrise became a reminder that His mercies are new every morning. Every act of kindness, every word of encouragement I shared, felt like planting another seed in the garden of my purpose. I knew there would still be challenges ahead, but I also knew that God's promise stood firm: He was making a way, even in the wilderness.

And this time, I was walking forward not as a woman broken by her past, but as one beautifully rebuilt by grace.

Transition vs. Transformation

There is a difference between transition and transformation. Transition is simply the act of moving from one stage to another. It is the physical shift from one place, role, or relationship to the next. Transformation, however, goes deeper. It is the renewing of the mind, the reshaping of the heart, and the refining of the soul.

Many people survive transitions but never embrace transformation. They change their appearance but remain stuck in the past internally. They change their surroundings but not their mindset. They relocate, remarry, or restart, yet carry the same pain and patterns into every new chapter. I knew I did not want that for my life. I had already lived enough of my story in survival mode. I wanted to live differently this time.

When God said, "See, I am doing a new thing," I realized that He was not just promising a change of circumstances. He was inviting me to become new on the inside. The "new thing" was not only about my future. It was about the woman I was becoming in the process.

The Process of Becoming

Transformation requires participation. God will open the door, but we must walk through it. He will plant the seed, but we must nurture it. That means facing uncomfortable truths and surrendering familiar patterns that no longer serve us. For me, that looked like confronting fears I had avoided for years.

I had to unlearn the belief that my worth was tied to my relationship status. I had to let go of the idea that I always had to be strong for everyone else. I had to admit that for a long time, I had measured myself by the approval of others. Transformation began when I stopped performing and started being honest.

Romans 12:2:"Do not conform to the pattern of this world, but be transformed by the renewing of your mind. Then you will be able to test and approve what God's will is: His good, pleasing, and perfect will."

That verse reminded me that transformation begins in the mind. It begins with changing how you think, how you speak, and how you see yourself. My thoughts had to align with what God said about me. My words had to reflect faith instead of fear. My heart had to release the lies that once held me hostage.

From Surviving to Thriving

Transition helps you move. Transformation helps you grow. During the early stages of healing, I was trying to survive. I wanted to stop hurting. I wanted to find my footing again. But as time passed, I began to sense that God was calling me to more. He was not content with me just surviving. He wanted me to thrive.

Thriving meant rediscovering joy. It meant stepping into purpose, not because everything was perfect, but because I had learned to trust God in imperfection. It meant saying yes to opportunities that once intimidated me and sharing my story without shame.

I began to see that my healing was not only for me. It was meant to help others find their way out of brokenness, too. Transformation turns pain into purpose. It gives meaning to what once felt meaningless. When God restores you, He equips you to restore others.

The Work of the Potter

Jeremiah 18:4 paints a beautiful picture of transformation: ***"But the pot He was shaping from the clay was marred in His hands; so the potter formed it into another pot, shaping it as seemed best to Him."***

That verse reminded me that even when I felt broken, I was still in God's hands. The cracks in my life did not disqualify me. They gave Him more places to pour in His grace. Every broken piece became part of His masterpiece.

Transformation is often slow and sometimes painful. The potter's wheel spins, and it can feel like your world is turning in circles. But every turn shapes you. Every pressure point has a purpose. God does not waste a single moment of your story.

When I finally surrendered to His process, I found peace. I stopped asking "Why me?" and started asking "What are you teaching me through this?" That simple shift changed everything. Instead of resisting the process, I began to trust it. I began to trust Him.

Transformation in Action

One of the most apparent signs of transformation is how you respond to life's challenges. Before, I would react out of fear or anger. Now, I pause and pray. I ask God for perspective before I respond. I do not always get it right, but I am learning.

Transformation taught me patience. It taught me that not every battle is mine to fight. It taught me to listen more and to speak less. It taught me to celebrate progress rather than demand perfection.

Every new opportunity became a chance to practice what I had learned. Whether it was leading a retreat, mentoring a young woman, or writing another chapter of my story, I brought a new mindset to it. I was no longer trying to prove my strength. I was walking in it.

Living as the New You

Transformation does not mean forgetting who you were. It means integrating who you were with who God is calling you to become. The old wounds no longer defined me, but they had shaped my compassion. The old mistakes no longer shamed me, but they had taught me humility. The old seasons no longer held me captive, but they had prepared me for leadership.

I began to live with purpose and intention. I stopped hiding from my past and started using it as a testimony. I no longer feared change because I had seen what God could do with a surrendered heart.

Philippians 1:6 "Being confident of this, that He who began a good work in you will carry it on to completion until the day of Christ Jesus." God had started a good work in me, and I knew He would finish it.

Transformation is not a single event. It is a lifelong journey of becoming who He created you to be.

The Beauty of Becoming

When I looked in the mirror, I no longer saw the same woman who once felt shattered by loss. I saw a woman shaped by grace, refined by faith, and empowered by love. I saw a woman who had learned that detours do not destroy God's plans. They are often discovered through them.

Transformation had changed how I saw everything. I no longer asked, "Why did this happen to me?" Instead, I began to say, "Thank You, Lord, for what You are doing through me." The pain had purpose. The waiting had wisdom. The breaking had birthed beauty.

Transition may move you into a new place, but transformation ensures that you arrive as a new person. And that is where true freedom lives: not in what changes around you, but in what changes within you.

A.R.E. Focus: Empower Your Future

When I reflect on everything I had walked through, I see how each season prepared me for the next. The storms that once broke me became the soil where purpose could grow. Every lesson, every tear, and every prayer became part of a divine design leading me toward empowerment.

The **A.R.E. Principle:** Acknowledge, Release, Empower, was born out of that revelation. It was not just a concept for others to follow. It was the roadmap I had lived. God took my story of heartbreak and turned it into a blueprint for healing and transformation.

Acknowledge: Recognize the Truth

Empowerment begins with honesty. You cannot heal from what you refuse to face. Acknowledging pain does not make you weak; it makes you courageous. When you name what hurt you, you take away its power to control you.

I had to acknowledge the anger, the fear, and the disappointment that lived deep inside me. I had to stop pretending I was fine when I was not. When I finally admitted the truth of my emotions before God, I felt the first wave of freedom wash over me.

Psalm 51:6 says, "Behold, You desire truth in the inward parts, and in the hidden part You make me to know wisdom." God honours our honesty. When we stop hiding, He begins His healing work.

Take time to reflect on what you need to acknowledge in your own life. Is it grief, resentment, guilt, or shame? Please write it down. Speak it aloud in prayer. Remember, acknowledgment is not about reliving pain. It is about recognizing it so you can release it.

Release: Let Go and Let God

Once you acknowledge the pain, the next step is to release it. This step is often the hardest because we become attached to what wounded us. We hold on to the memories, the questions, and the desire for justice. But holding on keeps us stuck. Releasing pain is not about forgetting. It is about trusting God to handle what we cannot.

Philippians 3:13 reminds us, "Forgetting what is behind and straining toward what is ahead, I press on toward the goal." Releasing means loosening your grip on the past so you can reach forward into your future.

For me, release looked like daily surrender. Some days, I had to lay the same burden down repeatedly. I let go of the need to understand everything. I released the bitterness that drained my energy. I released the guilt that whispered I had failed. Every time I let go, I made more space for peace.

Release is not a one-time act; it is a rhythm of trust. You release, and God restores. You let go, and He lifts you. The more you release, the lighter your spirit becomes.

Empower: Step Into Your New Identity

Empowerment is not about pretending to have it all together. It is about walking in the truth of who you are in Christ. When you acknowledge your pain and release what no longer serves you, you make room for God to empower you.

Empowerment means embracing your identity as a beloved child of God, created with purpose and equipped with everything you need to thrive. It is about replacing self-doubt with faith and fear with courage. It is about recognizing that your story has power.

Isaiah 61:3 says God gives "beauty for ashes, the oil of joy for mourning, and the garment of praise for the spirit of heaviness." That is empowerment. It is the divine exchange that happens when you let God take your brokenness and turn it into beauty.

For me, empowerment looked like stepping into new assignments with boldness. It meant saying yes to speaking engagements even when my voice trembled. It meant writing my book, *Shattered but Standing,* even when my story made me vulnerable. It meant mentoring women who were still in their own storms, showing them that healing was possible.

Empowerment does not mean the absence of fear. It

means moving forward despite it. It is walking by faith, trusting that God's strength will meet you at every step.

Practical Tool: The Empowerment Journal

To live empowered, you must stay connected to your source of strength—God. One of the most powerful tools for this journey is journaling. Set aside time each day to write in an Empowerment Journal. Divide it into three sections:

1. **Acknowledge:** Write what you are feeling honestly. No filters, no judgment.

2. **Release:** List what you are choosing to surrender to God today.

3. **Empower:** Declare who you are becoming through Christ. Write affirmations based on scripture and truth.

Example entry:

- *Acknowledge:* I feel anxious about the future.

- *Release:* I surrender my need to control the outcome.

- *Empower:* I am confident that God is working all things for my good.

Over time, you will look back at these entries and see your growth. You will see how God transformed your thoughts, healed your heart, and strengthened your spirit.

Living Empowered

Living empowered is not a destination; it is a daily choice. It means walking in gratitude, speaking life, and setting boundaries that protect your peace. It means knowing your worth and refusing to settle for less than God's best.

When you live empowered, you carry yourself differently. You speak with authority. You love without fear. You forgive faster. You serve with joy. You live with purpose.

Empowerment is not about perfection; it is about progress. Each day, you choose to align your thoughts with truth, your words with faith, and your actions with purpose.

As I continue my own journey, I am reminded that empowerment is not something you earn. It is a gift that flows from a healed heart and a surrendered life. God did not bring you this far to leave you. He is still doing a new thing in you.

Take courage, beloved. Stand tall in your story. You are no longer defined by what broke you, but by the One who restored you.

Declaration:
"I am a woman of purpose, walking in freedom, grounded in faith, and empowered by grace. My past does not limit me. My future is in God's hands."

The New Chapter Map

Practical steps help us move from theory to action. One way I embraced transformation was by creating a New Chapter Map.

- **Vision Board or Journal Page:** Create a space that reflects what you want this next season to look like. Include scriptures, images, words, and affirmations that inspire hope.

- **Milestone Markers:** Write down three short-term goals and one long-term goal. These serve as reminders that new chapters are built one step at a time.

- **Faith Anchors:** Choose two scriptures and one worship song that will steady you when fear or doubt tries to creep back in. Return to them whenever discouragement threatens to derail you.

This map reminded me that I was not wandering. God was giving me tools to chart a new path forward.

The Risk of Dreaming Again

One of the hardest parts, most complex, of stepping into a new chapter is allowing yourself to dream again. After profound loss, dreams can feel fragile, even dangerous. When you have experienced heartbreak or disappointment, the idea of hoping for something new can stir both excitement and fear. I remember asking myself, *What if it never happens? What if I am disappointed again?*

Dreams once came easily to me. I used to imagine a beautiful future filled with family, purpose, and peace. When my marriage ended, it felt like those dreams were buried under the rubble. Every time I thought about starting over, a voice whispered that it was safer not to hope. I convinced myself that if I did not dream, I could not be hurt.

But what I did not realize then was that refusing to

dream was another form of fear. I attempted to protect myself from pain, yet it was also keeping me from the fullness of life God had for me. Fear builds walls that feel like safety, but they eventually become prisons. I was alive, but not living. I was surviving, but not thriving.

God began to challenge me gently in that place. He reminded me that faith and fear cannot coexist. Faith invites us to step out of the boat, even when the waves are still rising. Faith calls us to see beyond what is broken and believe that beauty can grow again. I could feel God whispering to my heart, "Daughter, it is time to dream again."

Jeremiah 29:11 reminded me of His promise: "For I know the plans I have for you," declares the Lord, "plans to prosper you and not to harm you, plans to give you hope and a future." I had read that scripture countless times, but now it spoke to me differently. It was no longer a verse I quoted to others. It became a lifeline for my own spirit.

God's plans were not about harm. They were about hope. Even though the path had not been easy, I began to see that His purpose had never been to destroy me. Every closed door, every tear, and every detour had been shaping me for something greater. My role was to trust Him enough to pick up the pen and start dreaming again.

At first, my dreams were small. I dreamed of simple things: peace in my home, laughter returning to my days, the courage to travel, and the boldness to share my story. Then slowly, my dreams began to expand. I dreamed of helping women heal, of writing books that would remind others that God restores, and of creating spaces where hearts could find rest. Those dreams were planted in the soil of pain, but they grew because of faith.

Dreaming again required vulnerability. It meant opening my heart to possibilities that might not go as planned. It meant trusting God with outcomes I could not control. Yet the more I leaned into His guidance, the more I discovered that dreaming was not reckless; it was worship. Each dream was an act of surrender, a declaration that I believed in His goodness even after disappointment.

One of the most powerful truths I learned is that our dreams are not meant to replace God's plan; they are meant to align with it. When we invite Him into our desires, He refines them. Some dreams will flourish. Others may change shape. And a few may fade away to make room for something better. But no matter what, when we trust God with our dreams, we cannot lose.

Ephesians 3:20 declares that God "can do immeasurably more than all we ask or imagine, according to His power that is at work within us." That verse became a cornerstone for my new season. It reminded me that my imagination was only a glimpse of what God could do. He was not limited by my past or by what I thought was possible.

When I finally permitted myself to dream again, it felt like light entering a room that had been closed for too long. Hope began to stir. Ideas started flowing. My heart felt alive again. I realized that dreaming is not about controlling the future—it is about believing that the future is still worth showing up for.

To anyone afraid to dream again, I want to say this: you are not foolish for hoping. You are brave. Every dream you dare to hold in faith is a seed planted in the hands of a faithful God. Some seeds will take time to grow, but they will bloom in their season.

God is not finished writing your story. The same God who met you in your pain will meet you in your purpose. The same hands that held you through heartbreak will guide you into healing. Do not let fear have the final word. Trust Him, and dream again.

Reflection Exercise

Take a moment to sit with these questions. Write your answers in a journal.

- What is one dream I buried that I am ready to revive?

- What new opportunities has God placed before me that I have been hesitant to embrace?

- What practical step can I take this week to walk into my freedom and purpose?

- Who can I invite into this new chapter as a source of encouragement and accountability?

A Teachable Story

I remember meeting a woman at a retreat who shared that after her divorce, she never allowed herself to dream again. She poured all her energy into survival and routine. Day after day, she worked, provided for her family, and kept moving. But inside, she had given up hope that joy or fulfillment could ever be hers again.

One day, during a group session, someone asked her a simple question: *"What would you do if fear were not holding you back?"*

Tears filled her eyes as she whispered her answer. She had always dreamed of opening a small bakery. But she had buried that dream under layers of regret and responsibility. That moment of honesty cracked something open in her.

Months later, she sent a note to the group. She had started baking again, and her friends and neighbours loved her bread so much that she launched her business from her own kitchen. With each loaf of bread, she felt herself rise from the ashes of her past. What she thought was gone forever became the seed of her new chapter.

The lesson is this: sometimes the very thing you buried is waiting to become the foundation of your new season. God does not waste our gifts, and He does not let our dreams die without purpose.

The Courage to Risk

Dreaming again requires courage. It means risking disappointment. It means stepping into the unknown. But it also means stepping into possibility. Every dream, no matter how small, carries within it a spark of divine potential.

When Peter stepped out of the boat to walk on water, he risked sinking. Yet he also experienced something none of the others ever did: the miracle of walking toward Jesus on the waves. The story has always spoken deeply to me because it mirrors what it feels like to dream again after a season of pain. You know the waves are real. You can feel the wind against your face. Yet there is a pull in your spirit that says, *step out anyway.*

Dreams carry risk, but they also carry miracles. Without risk, there can be no revelation. Without stepping out, we never experience what faith can do.

In my own life, courage began in small steps. Starting new ventures, travelling again, and picking up my pen to write felt uncertain at first. I questioned whether anyone would care what I had to say or whether my story still mattered. But every time I chose to act despite fear, I discovered something extraordinary: God met me right where faith and fear collided.

Each act of courage became a seed of purpose. The retreats I now lead, the programs I design, and the books I write were all born from moments of trembling obedience. I did not feel ready. I said yes. Over time, I realized that courage is not the absence of fear. It is the decision to move forward in faith even when your knees are shaking.

Courage looks different for everyone. For some, it may be starting a new business. For others, it may be forgiving someone who deeply hurt them. For t is simply getting up each morning and choosing hope again. Courage is the daily decision to trust that what God has placed inside you is stronger than what stands against you.

Joshua 1:9 has become one of my favourite reminders: "Have I not commanded you? Be strong and courageous. Do not be afraid; do not be discouraged, for the Lord your God will be with you wherever you go." That verse reminds me that courage is not a suggestion. It is a divine invitation. It is God saying, *I know what lies ahead, and I will walk with you through it.*

When we take steps of faith, God does not promise that the path will be easy, but He promises His presence along the way. There were moments when I felt completely unqualified for what I was stepping into. I remember standing in front of a group of women at one of my first retreats, my heart racing, wondering if I truly had what it took to lead them. But as I spoke, I felt a peace settle over me. I realized that it was never about perfection. It was about obedience.

Courage calls us to move even when the outcome is uncertain. It teaches us to trust that every risk taken in faith will bear fruit in its time. Some seeds bloom quickly.

Others take years. But all grow under the light of God's faithfulness.

The more I embraced courage, the more I saw how God used each risk to build resilience. Travelling again reminded me that the world was bigger than my pain. Writing again reminded me that my voice still carried value. Launching new projects reminded me that I was capable of building something beautiful from broken pieces.

Courage also taught me humility. Sometimes, courage looks like leaping; it looks like staying still and trusting God to move on your behalf. It is not always about bold, public acts. Often, it is the quiet, unseen choices that shape our destiny.

There were seasons when courage meant saying yes. There were others when it meant saying no. I learned that courage is not about doing everything—it is about doing the right thing, the God thing, even when it costs you comfort.

Psalm 27:14 says, "Wait for the Lord; be strong and take heart and wait for the Lord." Waiting requires courage, too. It takes courage to believe that God is working behind the scenes when you cannot yet see the results.

Looking back, I see that every risk I took was worth it. Not because everything turned out exactly as I imagined, but because each step brought me closer to who God designed me to be. The courage to risk was the bridge between who I was and who I was becoming.

If you are standing at the edge of something new, I want to encourage you: step out. The water may look deep, but the One who calls you will not let you drown. Let faith be your compass and trust be your anchor. The world needs the gifts, the dreams, and the voice that only you can bring.

You may not feel ready, but you are equipped. You

may not know the outcome, but you know the One who holds it. Take the risk. Step out in faith. You might find that the miracle you have been praying for is waiting on the other side of your courage.

Daily Affirmations

1. My past does not define me.

2. God is writing a new story in my life.

3. I embrace transformation, not just transition.

4. My future is filled with hope, joy, and a sense of purpose.

5. I am not afraid to dream again.

Building a Legacy

A new chapter is not just about personal freedom. It is about building a legacy for those who come after you. My healing was never only about me. It was about those who would one day look at my life and see that God is faithful.

My children and grandchildren became part of my motivation to live fully again. I wanted them to see that storms do not end our stories. They refine them. I wanted them to understand that setbacks can become stepping stones when you trust God with the pieces. I wanted them to see that it is possible to rise, to rebuild, and to rejoice after heartbreak.

Psalm 145:4 says, "One generation commends your works to another; they tell of your mighty acts." That verse reminds me that our lives are testimonies meant to echo through generations. Every time we choose faith over fear, we are writing a story that speaks to those who will come after us.

When I think about legacy, I do not think about fame or fortune. I think about the lessons that live beyond me—the wisdom, the courage, and the faith that my family can draw from long after I am gone. Legacy is not built in a single grand moment. It is built on the small, consistent choices to trust God and to love people well.

For a long time, I believed that my pain disqualified me from leaving anything of value behind. I thought brokenness had ruined my ability to inspire others. But God reminded me that legacies are not built from perfection. They are built on redemption. He uses the cracks in our stories to let His light shine through.

When my grandchildren see me laugh again, travel again, and speak about hope, they are witnessing the fruit of God's healing power. When my daughters see me forgive and extend grace, they are learning what it means to walk in freedom. When my sons see me live with integrity and strength, they see that resilience is not weakness; it is worship.

I often reflect on **Deuteronomy 6:6–7, which says, "These commandments that I give you today are to be on your hearts. Impress them on your children**. Talk about them when you sit at home and when you walk along the road, when you lie down and when you get up." That scripture paints a picture of daily faithfulness: of passing on truth not through sermons, but through a lifestyle of consistency and love.

Building a legacy means being intentional about what we pour into others. It means telling the truth about where we have been and how God brought us through. It means not hiding the complex parts of our journey, because those are often the moments where His power is most evident.

I have learned that people do not connect with perfection. They connect with authenticity. My legacy is not in pretending that I never fell, but in showing that I got back up. It is in showing that God's grace is greater than our failures, and that His mercy meets us even when we least deserve it.

As I look at the work I do today—mentoring women, hosting retreats, writing books, and speaking words of life into those who feel forgotten—I see that every effort is a seed in the garden of legacy. Each conversation, each prayer, and each act of service becomes a testimony in motion. I am reminded that God does not waste anything. Every chapter of my life, even the painful ones, has become part of a larger story of restoration.

Legacy also means permitting others to heal. When a woman reads my story and realizes that she, too, can forgive, or when a young girl finds hope through one of my programs, that is a legacy. When a family is strengthened because someone learns to let go of resentment, it becomes a legacy. Legacy is not about how loudly we speak. It is about how deeply we impact hearts.

Proverbs 13:22 says, "A good person leaves an inheritance for their children's children." That inheritance is not just material wealth. It is spiritual strength, emotional resilience, and faith that endures. I desire to leave behind more than possessions. I want to leave behind a trail of purpose, a testimony of faith, and a blueprint of healing that others can follow.

Every time I stand before a group of women and share my story, I think of the generations listening beyond the room—the daughters, granddaughters, nieces, and young women who will one day face their own storms. I want them to know that healing is possible, forgiveness is powerful, and God's plans always lead to restoration.

Your legacy begins with the choices you make today. Whether you are raising children, leading a business, serving your community, or simply showing kindness to a neighbour, you are planting seeds that will grow into something eternal. The question is not whether you will leave a legacy, but what kind of legacy it will be.

As for me, I have decided that mine will be one of hope, faith, and forgiveness. My life may have been shattered at one point, but it now stands as a living testimony that beauty truly can rise from brokenness.

As I turn a new page in my life, I do so with gratitude. I do it for the generations who will one day tell the story: not of what I lost, but of what God restored.

The Gift of Community

Another lesson I learned in this season was the value of community. New chapters are not meant to be walked alone. Healing is deeply personal, but it is not meant to be solitary. God places people in our lives to encourage, challenge, and walk beside us on the journey.

When I first entered my season of rebuilding, I thought isolation was safety. I told myself that being alone meant I could not be hurt again. I built invisible walls around my heart and called them protection. But over time, those walls became prisons. They kept pain out, but they also kept love out.

God began to dismantle those walls gently. He sent people into my life who did not just see my smile; they saw my soul. These were people who spoke life when I could only speak defeat. Friends who prayed with me and for me. Mentors who reminded me of my worth when I doubted I had any, sisters in Christ who refused to let me settle for less than what God had promised.

Their presence was a gift. They did not try to fix me. They showed up. Sometimes healing comes not from answers, but from presence, the quiet assurance that you are not walking alone. Proverbs 27:17 says, "As iron sharpens iron, so one person sharpens another." God designed us to grow through connection.

I remember one evening when I was feeling especially loexceptionallyse felt heavy with silence, and grief crept back in like an uninvited guest. Then my phone rang. It was a friend from church. She did not ask for explanations. She said, "I felt led to call you. Let's pray." That prayer changed my night. It reminded me that community is one of God's most powerful tools for healing.

Healing may begin in solitude, but thriving happens in community. There is strength in shared stories. There is power in knowing that someone else has walked through similar pain and come out stronger. When you surround yourself with people who carry faith, their faith can lift you when yours feels weak.

Community also brings accountability. When I was tempted to shrink back into old habits of silence or fear, my sisters in Christ gently called me higher. They reminded me of the promises God had spoken over my life. They held me to my purpose when I wanted to give up. True community does not let you stay stuck in pain; it calls you forward into healing.

Ecclesiastes 4:9–10 says, "Two are better than one, because they have a good return for their labour. If eitlabourf them falls, one can help the other up." That is what a godly community does. It helps us rise. It reminds us that even when we fall, we are never too far gone for grace.

Out of my own healing came a desire to create that same kind of space for others. That is how **Healing the**

Heart was born. It started as a vision from God, a space where women devastated by broken relationships could find restoration through faith, forgiveness, and sisterhood.

At **Healing the Heart**, we laugh, we cry, we pray, and we grow together. It is not about pretending everything is perfect. It is about being real and allowing God to meet us in our authenticity. Women come with different stories—divorce, betrayal, grief, disappointment; but they all leave knowing they are not alone. They leave knowing that brokenness does not disqualify them; it refines them.

Community becomes a mirror that reflects both truth and grace. It shows you who you are in Christ and reminds you of what you are capable of. It provides strength when your own runs out and faith when yours feels fragile.

I often tell women who join my programs or attend my retreats that healing is not a straight path. There will be ups and downs, victories and setbacks. But when you have a community, you have people who will celebrate your victories and lift you during your setbacks. You have sisters who will pray for you, cheer you on, and remind you that God is still writing your story.

If you are in a season of rebuilding, do not isolate yourself. Seek out a community that offers. Surround yourself with people who speak life, who challenge you to grow, and who point you back to Jesus when you lose your way.

Community is not about perfection; it is about connection. It is about showing up for one another, sharing our stories, and holding space for grace to do its work.

Today, I can confidently say that I am standing because others stood with me. I am healed because others prayed for me. And I am thriving because I chose to open my heart to the gift of community.

So wherever you are in your journey, find your

people. Let them love you, pray for you, and walk with you. Because healing is not only about being made whole, it is also about helping others heal. Together rise.

A Teachable Moment: Beware of Distractions

As I mentioned earlier, I did fall in love again. Relationships can be beautiful gifts, but they can also be distractions if entered into without prayer and wisdom. A new chapter is not an invitation to fill emptiness with the wrong things. It is an invitation to let God lead.

Distractions can come in many forms: relationships, overwork, even busyness that numbs rather than heals. The key is to ask, "Is this drawing me closer to God's purpose, or pulling me away?"

Prayer

God, thank You for turning ashes into beauty. I release the past and embrace the new story you are writing in my life. Empower me to walk with courage, joy, and faith into the chapter ahead. Help me revive buried dreams and trust that Your plans for me are good. Surround me with community and wisdom. Guard me from distractions and lead me in purpose. Amen.

Closing Thought

Stepping into a new chapter does not erase the old one. It builds on it. The pain, the lessons, and the tears become part of the foundation. But they are not the whole story. You have survived the storm. You have walked through the fire. And now you are standing at the edge of something new.

This chapter is not about who you were. It is about who you are becoming. The past may have shaped you, but it does not limit you. The storm may have scarred you, but it did not stop you. The God who brought you through will lead you forward.

So step boldly into your new chapter. Dream again. Love again. Live again. Let your story become a testimony of transformation, not just transition. For God is always doing a new thing, and His story for you is still unfolding.

8.

WALKING IN PURPOSE DAILY

A new chapter does not simply begin because time has passed or circumstances have changed. A new chapter must be lived, written, and chosen one day at a time. Healing and freedom are not once-and-done experiences. They are daily decisions, sacred commitments to rise, to trust, and to hope again.

Each morning, when your feet touch the ground, you face a choice. You can dwell in yesterday's pain, replaying the wounds and regrets, or you can step boldly into today's purpose, trusting that God has given you another day filled with possibility. You may not know what the day holds, but you can be certain of who holds you.

Jesus reminds us in ***John 10:10, "I came that they may have life and have it abundantly."*** Abundance is not about possessions, status, or material wealth. It is about wholeness. It is about living with peace, joy, and a deep sense of meaning. True abundance flows from a heart that is surrendered, a mind that is renewed, and a spirit that knows where its hope comes from.

For a long time, I thought abundance meant everything had to be perfect before I could feel fulfilled. I needed to have every piece in place, my finances secure, my relationships restored, my dreams neatly unfolding, to experience the "abundant life." But God gently taught me that abundance is not found in perfection. It is found in the presence. It is discovered in those quiet moments when you feel His peace amid uncertainty and know, deep down, that you are still in His plan.

Abundance is waking up and being grateful that you are still here. It is finding joy in small victories. It is noticing beauty where you once only saw pain. It is laughter returning after years of tears. It is realizing that God's goodness is not something you will find at the end of the road. It is the very road you are walking.

Walking in purpose means aligning your daily steps with God's plan and refusing to let fear, discouragement, or doubt dictate your direction. It means surrendering the need to have every answer and choosing instead to trust the One who holds the answers. Some days you may walk confidently. Other days, you may take only one small, trembling step. But even that step, when taken in faith, moves you closer to the life God designed for you.

Romans 8:28 assures us that "all things work together for good to those who love God, to those who are called according to His purpose." That means nothing is wasted: not your pain, not your mistakes, not even your waiting. Every experience becomes part of the tapestry that God is weaving into your story.

Living your new chapter will require intention. It will ask you to make choices that align with healing and hope. You will need to speak life over yourself when old memories whisper lies. You will need to surround yourself with people who encourage your growth, not those who feed your fear. You will need to create moments of stillness so you can hear God's voice above the noise.

Abundance is not something you chase; it is something you cultivate. It grows as you nurture gratitude, walk in forgiveness, and keep your heart open to love again. It expands every time you serve others, every time you pray instead of worry, and every time you choose peace instead of chaos.

There will still be days when you stumble, when doubt knocks at your door, or when the past tries to pull you back. Do not be discouraged. The path of purpose is not a straight line. It is a journey of becoming, a daily unfolding of God's grace in your life. Each sunrise is another invitation to begin again.

Today, as you step into your new chapter, remember this: you do not walk alone. God is the author of your story, and He is still writing. The pages ahead are filled with lessons, laughter, and love you have not yet imagined. Let go of what no longer serves you. Lift your eyes toward what is ahead. Choose to live fully, to love deeply, and to walk in the abundance that Christ has already made available to you.

Your new chapter begins not when everything changes around you, but when something changes within you. When you decide to live with faith, gratitude, and courage, you become the living proof that beauty can rise from brokenness and that purpose can grow out of pain.

The Power of Daily Decisions

Purpose is not discovered in a single dramatic moment. It is revealed through the small, consistent choices you make every day. It is built one decision, one prayer, and one act of faith at a time.

Many people wait for a great revelation or a perfect opportunity before they begin to walk in purpose. They say things like, "When my situation changes, then I will start," or "When I feel ready, then I will take the next step." But purpose does not wait for perfect conditions. It begins right where you are, in the middle of imperfection.

Every sunrise is another opportunity to make choices that align with who God says you are. The words you speak, the thoughts you allow, the way you treat others, and the grace you extend to yourself are all part of the process. Healing is not just a feeling. It is a practice.

When I began to rebuild my life, I had to learn this truth for myself. I wanted to skip ahead to the big breakthrough moments: the visible victories that show the world I had overcome. But God was more interested in the quiet, unseen choices I made in the stillness of each morning.

He taught me that purpose grows in the soil of discipline. It grows when you choose prayer over panic. It grows when you open your Bible instead of opening the door to fear. It grows when you forgive again, even when the old wounds still ache. Purpose grows when you choose to love when bitterness would be easier, and when you take a step forward, even when you cannot see the whole path.

The Word of God gives us wisdom for these daily choices.***Proverbs 16:3 reminds us, "Commit to the Lord whatever you do, and He will establish your plans."*** When you surrender your plans to God, He brings alignment. He takes what looks ordinary and infuses it with eternal purpose.

Philippians 4:8 also teaches us where to focus our minds: "Whatever is true, whatever is noble, whatever is right, whatever is pure, whatever is lovely, whatever is admirable, if anything is excellent or praiseworthy—think about such things." Every day, we face countless thoughts. Not all of them deserve our attention. Choosing what to dwell on is one of the most powerful spiritual disciplines you can develop.

When your mind aligns with truth, your actions follow. What you meditate on shapes what you manifest. When you choose to focus on God's goodness, His promises, and His purpose, your life begins to reflect that light.

Daily Habits That Nurture Purpose

1. **Start with Gratitude.**
Before reaching for your phone or checking the news, take a moment to thank God for a new day. Gratitude shifts your perspective. It reminds you that every breath is a gift and every sunrise is another chance to walk in purpose.

2. **Feed Your Spirit.**
Spend time in God's Word, even if it is only one verse. Let scripture wash over your heart and renew your mind. God's Word is living and active. It strengthens you for whatever lies ahead.

3. **Speak Life Over Yourself.**
Proverbs 18:21 says, "The tongue has the power of life and death." Speak words that align with God's truth, not your fears. Replace "I can't" with "God can." Replace "I am not enough" with "I am chosen and equipped."

4. **Take Small, Faithful Steps.**
Do not wait for motivation to move. Begin with small steps. Send that email, make that call, take that class, start that prayer journal. Every step, no matter how small, is an act of obedience that moves you closer to your calling.

5. **Rest in God's Timing.**
Purpose unfolds in seasons. You may not see

fruit right away, but that does not mean God is not working. Seeds grow in silence before they break through the soil. Trust the process.

Scriptures for Strength

When you set out to live a life of purpose, you will need anchors. Life has a way of shaking us. Emotions rise, discouragement creeps in, and fear whispers lies. Without anchors, you drift. The Word of God is that anchor. It steadies you when the waves rise.

Here are scriptures that became pillars in my own journey:

- **Jeremiah 29:11 – *"For I know the plans I have for you," declares the Lord, "plans to prosper you and not to harm you, plans to give you hope and a future."***

- **Psalm 37:23 – *"The Lord orders the steps of a good man, and He delights in his way."***

- **Philippians 4:13 – *"I can do all things through Christ who strengthens me."***

- **Isaiah 41:10 – *"Fear not, for I am with you; be not dismayed, for I am your God. I will strengthen you; I will help you; I will uphold you with my righteous right hand."***

These verses are more than words. They are reminders that you are not walking alone. Your strength does not sustain your purpose, but by God's promises.

Daily Affirmations for Purpose

Words carry power. ***Proverbs 18:21 says, "Death and life are in the power of the tongue."*** Speaking truth over your life reshapes the way you think, believe, and act.

Here are affirmations I spoke over myself each morning to align my heart with God's truth:

- I am walking in God's plan for my life with confidence and peace.

- My past does not define me. God's promises define me.

- I release fear and embrace faith in every step I take.

- I am worthy of love, success, and joy because I am a child of God.

- Each day, I choose to live with intentionality, courage, and gratitude.

- My life is a testimony of healing, strength, and divine purpose.

- I am equipped for every challenge because Christ strengthens me.

-

At first, these statements felt awkward. I did not always believe them when I said them. But affirmations are not about what you feel in the moment. They are about declaring God's truth until your heart and mind catch up.

A Teachable Story: Purpose in Small Steps

At one of my retreats in Tobago, a young woman

shared with me that she felt completely stuck. She admitted that she had been waiting for her "big purpose" to arrive, believing her life would only have meaning once she had the perfect career or a clear, dramatic calling from God. In her eyes, everyone around her seemed to know exactly what they were meant to do, while she concluded she must have been overlooked.

I gently encouraged her to shift her perspective. Instead of waiting for something grand, what if she began with something small? I suggested she carve out just ten minutes each morning to read a scripture and write down one sentence of gratitude. It was simple. It was manageable. It was a seed.

Months later, she phoned me, her voice full of excitement. She said, "Because you allowed God to use your life and testimony at that retreat, I found the courage to start my own talk show on television." Her obedience in small steps had opened doors she never imagined. And what a blessing it was to sit across from her as a guest on that very show when I returned to Tobago a few months later.

Her story is proof that purpose does not arrive in one dramatic moment. It unfolds gradually through small, faithful choices that align your heart with God's will.

The lesson is simple but powerful: never underestimate the impact of daily choices. They may seem small, but they are the building blocks of your destiny.

Teachable Moment: Purpose Is Built, Not Found

We often think of purpose as something to find, like a hidden treasure buried somewhere out of reach. But the truth is, purpose is something you build with God's help. It is formed through your faith, your choices, and your perseverance.

Every act of obedience adds a brick to the foundation

of your purpose. Every moment of surrender lays another stone. Over time, what once looked like fragments of your life becomes a masterpiece in God's hands.

The Battle of Consistency

One of the most significant challenges in living a new chapter is not starting, but staying consistent. The beginning is exciting. You set goals, make plans, and feel energized by the idea of change. But the actual test of transformation is not in the beginning. It is continuing.

Enthusiasm can carry you through the first few days or weeks, but real growth requires endurance. There will be mornings when motivation is nowhere to be found. There will be days when you wonder if your efforts are even making a difference. But it is in those moments, when you choose to keep showing up, that purpose deepens, and character is formed.

Galatians 6:9 reminds us, "Let us not grow weary in doing good, for in due season we shall reap, if we do not lose heart." This verse taught me that consistency is not about rushing the process. It is about trusting that every seed of obedience, no matter how small, is producing fruit in its season.

When I began rebuilding my life, I wanted quick results. I wanted to see evidence that healing was working, that faith was paying off, that the new life I was trying to create was taking shape. But God was not in a hurry. He was more interested in building depth than speed.

Consistency is what builds that depth. It is what anchors your faith when emotions fluctuate. It teaches you that God's promises are not dependent on your feelings. Even when you cannot see immediate results, He is working behind the scenes. Every prayer you pray, every act of faith, and every moment you choose peace over panic becomes part of your harvest.

Think of a farmer planting seeds. The soil looks quiet for a while. There are no visible signs of growth. But underneath the surface, life is developing. Roots are forming. That hidden work is essential. Without it, the plant would not survive the storms that come later. In the same way, your consistency allows spiritual roots to grow deep enough to sustain you through the seasons ahead.

Living purposefully means showing up even when it feels ordinary. It means reading your Bible on days when you feel disconnected. It means praying when you do not have fancy words, just a whisper of "Lord, help me." It means choosing kindness when frustration feels easier. These are not small acts: they are sacred ones. They prove that your faith is more than a feeling; it is a way of life.

Distractions will always come. Sometimes they appear as opportunities that look good but are not aligned with your purpose. Other times, they show up as doubt, fatigue, or comparison. The enemy loves to plant the thought that consistency is not worth it—that no one sees your effort, that you are not making progress, that it would be easier to quit. But God sees. Every quiet act of obedience matters to Him.

1 Corinthians 15:58 says, "Therefore, my dear brothers and sisters, stand firm. Let nothing move you. Always give yourselves fully to the work of the Lord, because you know that your labour in the Lord is not in vain."

Your consistency is never wasted. Even when it feels unnoticed, it is building spiritual strength. It is preparing you for doors that have not yet opened. It is shaping you into the person who can carry the blessings you have prayed for.

There were seasons when I wanted to give up on writing, on ministry, even on myself. I questioned whether my efforts mattered. But every time I stayed consistent, every time I chose to show up again, God met me there. He reminded me that His faithfulness is revealed through my willingness to keep going.

Consistency does not mean never stumbling. It means getting back up when you do. It means learning to rest without quitting. Rest is not failure. It is part of sustainability. Even Jesus withdrew to pray and recharge. You cannot pour from an empty vessel.

The secret to lasting consistency is grace. You are not doing this in your own strength. ***Philippians 2:13 says, "For it is God who works in you to will and to act to fulfill His good purpose."*** That means you are not walking this path alone. God gives you both the desire and the ability to keep moving forward.

Reflection Exercise

Ask yourself these questions:

- In what area of my life do I struggle most with consistency?

- What distractions or discouragements pull me away from my focus?

- What daily or weekly routine can I put in place to help me stay steady?

- How can I remind myself that God is working even when I cannot see progress?

Write your reflections and pray over them. Ask God to strengthen your commitment and to give you joy in the process, not just the outcome.

Daily Practice: Your Purpose Path

Try this simple practice each evening for one week:

1. Write down one choice you made today that aligned with your purpose.

2. Thank God for giving you the strength to take that step.

3. Ask Him to guide you to one purposeful choice tomorrow.

This practice enables you to see progress in real-time. Over weeks and months, these small steps create momentum.

Teachable Moment: Overcoming Distractions

Living with purpose does not mean life will suddenly become easy. You will face distractions. They may come in the form of relationships, overwork, fear, or even opportunities that are good but not aligned with God's will for you.

Not every open door is your assignment. Not every opportunity is meant for you. Discernment is key. Ask yourself:

- Does this draw me closer to God's purpose for me, or pull me away?

- Does this bring peace, or does it stir confusion?

- Will this strengthen me, or drain me?

Purposeful living requires saying no as often as saying yes. Your 'no' creates space for the right 'yes'.

A.R.E. Focus: Empower Daily Choices

The A.R.E. framework applies not only to healing but to purposeful living.

- **Acknowledge:** Recognize the habits, thoughts, and choices that either move you toward or away from your purpose.

- **Release:** Let go of fear, perfectionism, or the need for immediate results. Trust God's timing.

- **Empower:** Choose daily practices that align with God's truth and build strength for your future.

Building Momentum

Think of daily choices like laying bricks. One by one, they may not look like much. But as days and weeks pass, the structure of a new life begins to take shape. The prayers you whisper, the scriptures you memorize, the affirmations you repeat, the small steps you take toward your goals: all of these build something that lasts.

Momentum is built through repetition. Every step of faith, no matter how small, creates movement. And once you start moving, it becomes easier to keep going. Forward motion does not come from giant leaps, but from steady, intentional progress. You do not need to run to make progress. You need to keep walking.

When I first began rebuilding my life, I underestimated the power of consistency. I thought significant changes required big actions. But over time, I realized it was the small, faithful habits: the quiet prayers before dawn, the moments of gratitude, the scriptures written on sticky notes- that carried me forward. Momentum was not about speed. It was about staying connected to purpose.

Isaiah 40:31 became my encouragement during this time: "But they who wait for the Lord shall renew their strength; they shall mount up with wings like eagles; they shall run and not be weary; they shall walk and not faint." That verse reminded me that progress is not always visible, but it is always happening when you lean on God. Waiting is not wasted time when it is time spent trusting Him.

The Power of Habit

Momentum grows when faith becomes a rhythm. When you begin your mornings with prayer, your heart becomes anchored before the day begins. When you end your nights with gratitude, your mind rests in peace instead of anxiety. These daily anchors create stability in seasons of change.

Proverbs 4:25-27 encourages us, "Let your eyes look straight ahead; fix your gaze directly before you. Give careful thought to the paths for your feet and be steadfast in all your ways. Do not turn to the right or the left; keep your foot from evil." This scripture reminds us that focus fuels progress. When you fix your eyes on your purpose and keep walking, momentum builds naturally.

The enemy loves to use distraction to steal momentum. He whispers thoughts like, "You are not moving fast enough," or "You have failed before, so why try again?" But each time you ignore those lies and take another step in faith, you break his hold. God honours persistence, not perfection.

Teachable Moment: Progress Over Perfection

One of the lessons I learned in this season was that perfection is the enemy of progress. Often, we stop because things do not look as we imagined. We compare our journey to others and convince ourselves we are behind. But God measures growth differently. He values obedience more than outcomes.

You may not see immediate results, but that does not mean nothing is happening. Just like a seed planted beneath the soil, your faith is developing roots. The roots must grow deep before fruit appears. Momentum builds quietly, below the surface, long before it becomes visible.

Practical Ways to Build Momentum

1. **Start Small, Stay Faithful**
   Choose one area of your life where you want to grow. Commit to a small, achievable action each day. It might be five minutes of prayer, reading one psalm, or journaling one paragraph. Small steps create lasting habits.

2. **Celebrate Progress, Not Just Results**
   Each step you take is evidence that you are moving forward. Take time to thank God for progress, no matter how small. Celebration fuels motivation.

3. **Guard Your Focus**
   Stay aware of what drains your energy and what feeds your faith. Replace distractions with disciplines that align with your purpose.

4. **Invite Accountability**
   Share your goals with someone who encourages you. Momentum grows stronger when you walk with others who share your values.

5. **Rest Intentionally**

Momentum does not mean constant motion. Even God rested on the seventh day. Rest replenishes your energy so you can keep building without burning out.

Reflection Exercise
Ask yourself:

- What small daily habit is helping me move forward right now?

- What distractions or fears keep me from maintaining momentum?

- How can I remind myself of progress when results seem slow?

Write these reflections down and pray over them. Ask God to renew your strength and to give you endurance for the journey ahead.

Closing the Gap Between Intention and Action

Many of us live with good intentions. We intend to pray more. We intend to exercise. We intend to forgive, to dream again, to live with purpose. But intentions without action create frustration. They keep us stuck in cycles of waiting, wishing, and wondering when life will change.

The truth is, change does not come through intention alone. It comes through obedience. It comes through the willingness to act even when you do not feel ready. Closing the gap means moving from wishing to doing. It means committing to one small step today instead of waiting for the perfect conditions tomorrow.

James 1:22 reminds us, "Do not merely listen to the word, and so deceive yourselves. Do what it says."

Obedience is action. Purpose is lived out, not just imagined. Hearing the truth is not enough; it must be put into practice. Faith without works is like a seed that is never planted: it carries potential but never bears fruit.

The Trap of Waiting for "When"

Many people live in what I call the "when zone."

When I have more time, then I will start.

When I feel stronger, then I will forgive.

When I am more confident, then I will pursue my dream.

But "when" is a delay tactic disguised as wisdom. The perfect time rarely comes. God often calls us to act while conditions remain uncertain, because it is in the act of obedience that faith grows. The Israelites did not see the Red Sea part before stepping forward. They had to walk toward it in faith.

When you choose to act on God's word, you invite His power into your circumstances. The step comes before the strength. The obedience comes before the breakthrough.

From Intention to Implementation

Closing the gap between intention and action begins with clarity. Ask yourself, *What is one thing I know God is asking me to do right now?* Maybe it is time to start writing the book, reach out to that person, join the church group, or forgive someone who hurt you. Whatever it is, start small but start now.

Ecclesiastes 11:4 warns, "Whoever watches the wind will not plant; whoever looks at the clouds will not reap." If you wait for everything to line up perfectly, you will miss the opportunity to move forward—God honours movement.

Teachable Moment: Faith Requires Motion

Faith is not passive. It is active trust in God's promises. When you step out in faith, even with trembling hands, you show that your confidence is not in your ability but in His faithfulness.

Think of Peter stepping out of the boat. He could have stayed seated, analyzing the waves, debating whether it was safe. Instead, he acted on Jesus' word and walked on water. Was it perfect? No. Did he sink for a moment? Yes. But Peter experienced a miracle that no one else did because he was willing to move.

Your miracle, your breakthrough, your next level of growth: it is on the other side of action.

Practical Ways to Close the Gap

1. **Define One Clear Step.**
   Do not overwhelm yourself with ten goals. Choose one thing you can act on today. Progress begins with focus.

2. **Create Accountability.**
   Tell someone you trust what step you are taking. Accountability transforms intention into follow-through.

3. **Replace Excuses with Empowerment.**
   Instead of saying, "I can't right now," ask, "What can I do right now?" Small steps still move you forward.

4. **Celebrate Every Act of Obedience.**
   Each time you take action, no matter how small, thank God for giving you courage. Gratitude keeps momentum alive.

Reflection Exercise

- What intention in my life has stayed on hold for too long?

- What fear or excuse has been keeping me from acting?

- What one step of faith can I take this week to close the gap?

Write your reflections in your journal and pray over them. Ask the Holy Spirit to guide your actions and give you clarity and boldness.

Daily Affirmations

- I am moving from intention to action through faith.

- I no longer wait for perfect conditions; I trust God's timing.

- My obedience today will unlock blessings tomorrow.

- I am bold, focused, and committed to walking in purpose.

- Every step I take in faith pleases God and shapes my future.

Prayer

Lord, thank you for reminding me that each day is a gift and an opportunity to walk in the purpose for which You created me. Please help me choose life, faith, and joy over fear and discouragement. Strengthen me to be consistent in my daily walk and let my life be a light that reflects Your love. Guide my steps, protect me from distractions, and give me courage to live fully in this new chapter. Amen.

Closing Thought

Intentions are the seeds of change, but only action allows them to grow. You cannot build a new life on plans alone. You must move. You must trust God enough to do the next right thing, even when it feels small.

Do not let fear or perfectionism delay your destiny. The door to your next season is unlocked by obedience. Take the step, and watch how God multiplies it.

9.

THE 7-DAY PURPOSE CHALLENGE

Healing and transformation rarely happen in a single dramatic moment. More often, they unfold through steady, intentional choices. It is the decision you make each morning. It is the prayer you whisper when your thoughts feel heavy. It is the act of aligning your heart with God's truth when everything around you is trying to convince you otherwise.

One of the most powerful ways to step into your new season is by establishing rhythms of scripture, affirmation, reflection, and prayer. When you anchor your days in God's Word and speak His truth over your life, you train your mind and heart to walk in His promises.

This **7-Day Purpose Challenge** is designed to help you build those rhythms. Each morning, set aside a few minutes to read the scripture, declare the affirmation aloud, reflect on the prompt, and end with a prayer of gratitude. These small daily choices will begin to shift your perspective. Over time, they will strengthen your confidence in God's plan and empower you to walk boldly in your purpose.

Day 1: God's Plans Are Good

Scripture
"For I know the plans I have for you," declares the Lord,

"plans to prosper you and not to harm you, plans to give you hope and a future." (Jeremiah 29:11)

Affirmation

I trust God's plan for my life, and I know my future is secure in Him.

Reflection Prompt

What part of my life do I need to surrender to God's plan today?

Devotional Thought

Jeremiah 29:11 is a verse many of us are familiar with, but it is often misunderstood. The context of this promise was spoken to a people living in exile. They were far from home, their dreams were shattered, and their future felt uncertain. Yet in the middle of despair, God reminded them: His plans were still good.

This truth is timeless. Your situation may not look like what you prayed for. It may feel messy or painful. But God's plan is not cancelled by your circumstances. His plan is one of hope and a future. The first step in living on purpose is surrendering your timeline and expectations to Him.

Practical Example

When I first faced divorce, I could not imagine that God still had good plans for me. My dreams of family had collapsed, and the future seemed like an empty page. But slowly, as I surrendered my story into His hands, He began to reveal new assignments. Coaching women, writing, and speaking were not things I had planned, but they were part of the future He had prepared for me.

Prayer

Lord, I entrust my fears about the future to Your care. Help me trust that Your plans for me are good, even when I cannot see them. Teach me to surrender every detail and walk in confidence that You hold my tomorrow. Amen.

Day 2: Ordered Steps

Scripture
"The Lord orders the steps of a good man, and He delights in his way." (Psalm 37:23)
Affirmation
God's wisdom and direction guide each step I take today.
Reflection Prompt
Where do I sense God is leading me right now?
Devotional Thought
Purpose is not a giant leap. It is revealed one step at a time. We often want God to show us the entire map, but He delights in guiding us step by step. This requires trust.

Your responsibility is not to know the whole plan. Your responsibility is to take the step He places before you today. Maybe it is a phone call you need to make, a book you need to read, or a quiet prayer you need to pray.
Practical Example
I once met a woman who longed to write her story but never started because she did not know how the book would end. I reminded her that she did not need the ending yet—she only needed the first step. She began journaling daily, and in time, those pages grew into a manuscript.
Prayer
Father, thank You for ordering my steps. Help me not to rush ahead or lag, but to walk in sync with Your leading. Remind me that even small steps matter when you guide them. Amen.

Day 3: Strength in Christ

Scripture

"I can do all things through Christ who strengthens me."
(Philippians 4:13)

Affirmation

I have the strength for every challenge because Christ lives in me.

Reflection Prompt

What challenge do I need to approach with faith instead of fear?

Devotional Thought

This verse is often quoted, but its power lies in context. Paul wrote it while imprisoned. His strength did not come from circumstances; it came from Christ within him.

When life feels overwhelming, remember this: strength is not the absence of struggle. Strength is the presence of Christ in the struggle. You are not expected to face challenges alone. His Spirit empowers you to rise, endure, and overcome.

Practical Example

When I first stepped into public speaking after my divorce, I was terrified. My voice shook, my hands trembled, and I wondered if I could even stand on the stage. Yet each time, I whispered Philippians 4:13. With every word, I felt God's strength hold me.

Prayer

Lord, thank You that my strength does not come from myself but from Christ living in me. Teach me to rely on Your power when I feel weak. Remind me that Your strength is made perfect in my weakness. Amen.

Day 4: Courage Over Fear

Scripture

"Fear not, for I am with you; be not dismayed, for I am

your God. I will strengthen you; I will help you, I will uphold you with my righteous right hand." (Isaiah 41:10)

Affirmation

I release fear and walk boldly in the confidence of God's presence.

Reflection Prompt

What fear do I need to replace with faith today?

Devotional Thought

Fear is loud. It tells you that you cannot, you are not enough, and you will fail. But God's presence is louder. The antidote to fear is not courage alone. It is knowing that you are not walking alone.

Practical Example

I remember a season when I hesitated to make financial decisions after my divorce because fear gripped me. But each time I stepped forward in faith, God provided for me. Fear whispered lack, but His presence reminded me of provision.

Prayer

Lord, I thank You for being with me in every moment. Replace my fears with faith. Help me to walk boldly, knowing Your hand upholds me. Amen.

Day 5: A New Creation

Scripture

"If anyone is in Christ, he is a new creation; the old has gone, the new is here." (2 Corinthians 5:17)

Affirmation

I am renewed, restored, and empowered by God's Spirit.

Reflection Prompt

What old mindset or label do I need to release?

Devotional Thought

Your identity is not in your past. It is not your mistake. It is not in the labels others have given you. In Christ, you are new. Transformation is not about fixing the old; it is about becoming something brand new.

Practical Example

For years, I carried the label of "divorced woman" like a scarlet letter. But God reminded me that my true identity was "beloved daughter." The moment I embraced that truth, shame began to lose its grip.

Prayer

Lord, thank You that my past does not define me. I am a new creation in Christ. Help me release every old label and walk boldly in my true identity. Amen.

Day 6: God's Love Never Fails

Scripture

"Nothing can separate us from the love of God that is in Christ Jesus our Lord." (Romans 8:38-39)

Affirmation

God deeply loves me, and nothing can take that away.

Reflection Prompt

How can I remind myself of God's love throughout today?

Devotional Thought

God's love is not fragile or conditional. It is not based on your performance or perfection. It is steady, constant, and unshakable. Even when you doubt, fail, or fall short, His love remains.

Practical Example

There were nights when loneliness consumed me, and I wondered if I was truly loved. But as I meditated on Romans 8, I realized that nothing, neither my divorce, my mistakes, nor my fears, could separate me from His love.

Prayer

Father, thank You for Your unfailing love. Help me rest in

the truth that nothing can separate me from You. Remind me today of Your love in every detail. Amen.

Day 7: Abundant Life

Scripture
"I came that they may have life and have it abundantly."
(John 10:10)

Affirmation
I live a full, joyful, and purposeful life through Christ.

Reflection Prompt
How will I choose abundance today in my thoughts, actions, or words?

Devotional Thought
Abundance is not about wealth or possessions. It is about fullness of heart, joy, and peace that only Christ can give. Choosing abundance means deciding to focus on God's goodness, even when life feels uncertain.

Practical Example
I once believed that abundance was out of reach for me after my marriage ended. But I discovered abundance in laughter with friends, in moments of worship, and in the quiet joy of walking along the beach. Abundance was not about what I lost but about the presence of God filling what remained.

Prayer
Lord, thank You for the gift of abundant life in Christ. Please help me cultivate joy, peace, and purpose every day. Teach me to see abundance not in things, but in You. Amen.

Closing Encouragement

Seven days may not change your entire life, but they can begin to shift your heart. These scriptures, affirmations, and reflections are seeds. When planted daily, they grow into faith, resilience, and a sense of purpose. Over time, they rewire your thoughts, strengthen your confidence, and remind you of who you are in Christ.

Do not stop after seven days. Return to these truths often. Create your own weekly rhythms with fresh scriptures and affirmations. Invite accountability by sharing the challenge with a friend or small group.

Walking in purpose is not about perfection. It is about choosing, each day, to align your heart with God's truth and to step forward in faith. Your destiny is not built in one dramatic moment; it is built through consistent, daily choices to live fully in the love and promises of God.

10.

FINISHING STRONG

There comes a moment in every journey when you realize you are no longer who you were. The pain that once consumed you has lost its power, and the tears that once blurred your vision now water the soil of your growth. It is in that moment that you understand that survival was never the goal. God did not bring you through the fire to survive. He brought you through so that you could stand stronger, wiser, and ready to live fully again.

Finishing strong is not about perfection or arrival. It is about remaining faithful to the process even when the road is long. It is about trusting that God, who started the work in you, will be faithful to complete it. Every step, every tear, every prayer, and every quiet act of obedience have been leading you here: to this season where purpose begins to unfold.

When I look back on the path behind me, I see how every storm carried a lesson, every heartbreak built endurance. Every delay prepared me for something more profound. At the time, I could not see it. I only saw the pain. But God was doing something I could not yet perceive. He was teaching me to finish strong.

The Weight of Weariness

There were seasons when I felt weary down to my bones. I had fought through heartbreak, forgiven those who wounded me, and started rebuilding my life piece by piece. But weariness can creep in quietly, even after healing begins. There were days when I wondered if I had anything left to give. I had learned to stand again, but standing takes strength, and strength requires renewal.

Galatians 6:9 became my reminder: "Let us not grow weary in doing good, for in due season we shall reap if we do not lose heart." Those words held me when exhaustion whispered that it was easier to stop.

Sometimes the most brutal battles are not fought in chaos but in the quiet: the moments when no one sees the effort it takes to keep showing up. When the applause fades and the routine feels heavy, that is where perseverance is built. Finishing strong means pushing through the ordinary with extraordinary faith.

The Slow Work of God

God does not rush healing, nor does He rush growth. The process of finishing strong is often slow, deliberate, and sacred. It requires you to trust His timing when nothing seems to move fast enough. I had to learn that progress is not always visible. Some of God's most significant work happens beneath the surface, where roots grow deep before fruit appears.

There were times when I felt stuck, as if my life had stalled. I prayed for a breakthrough, yet God kept me in a season of quiet preparation. Looking back now, I see that He was fortifying me. He was strengthening my faith so that when new doors opened, I would be ready to walk through them with confidence and humility.

Isaiah 40:31 reminds us, "But they that wait upon the Lord shall renew their strength; they shall mount up with wings as eagles; they shall run and not be weary, and they shall walk and not faint." Waiting is not wasted when it is done in faith. It is the training ground for endurance.

The Power of Faithful Steps

Finishing strong does not happen through one grand

act. It happens through countless small acts of faith. Each time you pray when you feel dry, you build strength. Each time you forgive when it still hurts, you grow. Each time you show up when it would be easier to quit, you gain ground.

There were mornings when I had to speak life over myself. I would look in the mirror and say, "You have come too far to turn back now." It was not arrogance. It was in agreement with God's promise. The same God who carried me through my darkest season was still carrying me.

Every day was a choice to believe that purpose still waited on the other side of perseverance. Some days that meant writing when inspiration was gone. On other days, it meant encouraging someone else even while I was still healing. What I discovered is that God multiplies strength when you pour out what you have left.

When I encouraged others, I found myself renewed. When I served, I found joy. When I gave thanks for small things, I discovered peace. Those small, faithful steps became the building blocks of endurance.

The Temptation to Stop

There were moments I wanted to stop. I had achieved a measure of peace and stability, and part of me wondered if that was enough. Why keep pressing forward? Why dream bigger? Why risk disappointment again?

But deep down, I knew the journey was not finished. God was still writing my story. Stopping early would have meant missing the fullness of what He was preparing. There is always a temptation to settle when comfort returns. But comfort can become captivity if you stay too long.

Finishing strong means pushing beyond comfort zones and trusting that God's vision for your life is larger than your fear. The same God who healed your heart also wants to use that healed heart to bring hope to others. Your story carries power, but only if you keep walking.

The Refining Fire

Endurance is shaped through refining. There are seasons when God allows fire not to destroy, but to purify. It is in those fiery seasons that our motives are tested, our faith is deepened, and our character is shaped.

I remember a time when I faced betrayal again, long after I thought I had mastered forgiveness. My first reaction was disbelief. I cried out, "Lord, not again!" But God showed me that this was not a setback. It was a test. Would I respond the way I once did, or would I stand in grace?

Every challenge that arises after healing is not an attack. Sometimes it is confirmation that you have grown. The things that once shattered you no longer have the same power over you. You may feel the sting, but you no longer crumble. That is a strength. That is finishing strong.

Zechariah 13:9 says, "I will refine them like silver and test them like gold. They will call on my name, and I will answer them. I will say, 'They are my people,' and they will say, 'The Lord is our God.'" Refining is God's way of revealing what He has placed inside you. The gold is always there; the fire brings it to the surface. I remember singing and recording "Refiner's Fire," not knowing that God would lead me through the fire in that season of my life. It was painful, but worth it.

Endurance in Purpose

When I started leading retreats and coaching women, I realized how vital endurance truly is. People often see the fruit but not the roots. They see the speaking engagements, the books, the conferences, but they do not see the nights of prayer, the moments of doubt, or the tears behind closed doors.

Endurance is what keeps you standing when results

take time. It keeps you faithful to your calling when progress feels hidden. It keeps you anchored when criticism comes.

To finish strong means to honour your assignment, even when it is hard. It means doing what God asked you to do when no one applauds. It means trusting that your obedience matters even when you do not see immediate reward. God's favour often shows up after seasons of unseen faithfulness.

Grace for the Journey

There were times I leaned heavily on grace because I had nothing else. Grace met me when I failed. Grace covered me when I fell short. Grace reminded me that strength was not about striving. It was about surrender.

2 Corinthians 12:9, "My grace is sufficient for you, for my power is made perfect in weakness." Those words became my reminder that God never required perfection, only presence. He wanted me to stay in the race, even when my pace slowed.

Finishing strong means understanding that grace is not a safety net for failure; it is the fuel for forward motion. Grace empowers us to rise, to keep going, and to believe again.

Finishing with Faith

There will always be unfinished dreams, unanswered prayers, and roads that stretch beyond what you can see. But faith allows you to finish strong even when you do not have all the answers. Faith says, "I trust You, God, even when I do not understand."

Faith is what allows you to look at your past without regret, your present without fear, and your future with hope. It is what sustains you when strength fades and what lifts you when discouragement sets in.

Hebrews 12:1–2 says, "Let us run with perseverance

the race marked out for us, fixing our eyes on Jesus, the pioneer and perfecter of faith." The race is not about competition. It is about completion. Keep your eyes on Jesus, and you will always find your stride.

Leaving a Legacy of Strength

Finishing strong is not just for you. It is for those who are watching. My children and grandchildren have watched me walk through valleys and climb mountains. They have seen tears, victories, and prayers. My endurance became their example. My perseverance showed them what faith looks like when life gets hard.

Psalm 145:4 says, "One generation shall commend your works to another and shall declare your mighty acts." When you finish strong, you leave a legacy that outlives your lifetime. You permit others to keep rising.

I want my life to tell a story of grace. I want others to know that storms do not define us; how we rise after them does. Finishing strong means walking in purpose until the very end, knowing that each chapter, joyful or painful, was part of God's design.

The Gift of Still Standing

When I look back now, I see that finishing strong was never about crossing a finish line. It was about discovering that I could still stand, still love, still hope. It was about realizing that every ending is also a beginning in God's hands.

I have learned that strength is not measured by how loudly you roar but by how quietly you trust. It is found in the steady rhythm of faith, the courage to keep showing up, and the peace of knowing that you are exactly where God wants you to be.

Every scar carries a story, and every story carries a lesson. My scars remind me of the battles I have fought, but they also testify to God's faithfulness. I am still standing, not because I am strong, but because His grace never let me fall too far.

Reflection: The Faithful Finisher

If you are reading these words and feel weary, remember this: you are not finished yet. God is not done writing your story. You may be in the middle of a chapter that feels uncertain, but the Author knows the ending. Do not give up. Do not let fear convince you that you have reached your limit.

You are closer to a breakthrough than you realize. The strength you need is already inside you. The same Spirit that raised Jesus from the dead lives in you. That power gives you the ability to finish strong, no matter how the story began.

When life feels heavy, whisper this prayer:
"Lord, give me the strength to keep walking, even when I feel weak. Remind me that you are not finished with me. Help me to finish this chapter of my life with grace, faith, and peace. Let my endurance reflect Your glory."

Then take the next step. One act of faith. One moment of gratitude. One decision to keep going.

Because finishing strong is not about reaching perfection, it is about remaining faithful until the very end.

Final Reflection Prayer and Declaration

"He who began a good work in you will carry it on to completion." – Philippians 1:6

A Prayer for Finishing Strong

Heavenly Father,

Thank You for walking with me through every storm, every valley, and every tear that brought me here.

Thank you for being my constant anchor when life felt uncertain and my strength when I had none left.

Today, I choose to let go of every weight that has held me back.

I lay down the burdens of regret, the chains of unforgiveness, and the fears that whisper I am not enough.

I receive Your grace that reminds me I am still Yours, still loved, still chosen, and still called.

Teach me to finish strong.

When I am tired, remind me of Your promises.

When I am afraid, remind me that You are my refuge.

When I doubt my worth, remind me that I am Your masterpiece, fearfully and wonderfully made.

Lord, I ask You to breathe new life into my dreams.

Help me to walk boldly into the new season You have prepared for me.

Let my story bring hope to others.

Let my scars testify to Your healing.

Let my life reflect Your grace in every word, every choice, and every act of love.

I declare that I am not defined by what I lost but by what I have gained through You.

You have turned my mourning into dancing, my despair into peace, and my weakness into strength.

Today, I close this chapter with gratitude.

And I step into the next with courage, faith, and expectation.

In Jesus' Name,

Amen.

Declaration: I Am Finishing Strong

Speak this over yourself aloud each morning for the next seven days.

- I am no longer broken. I am becoming whole.

- I am not who I was. I am who God says I am.

- I walk in grace, not guilt.

- I live with purpose, not fear.

- I choose peace over bitterness, faith over doubt, and joy over despair.

- I finish what God started in me with strength, love, and endurance.

- I am **shattered but standing**, healed and whole in Christ.

Reflection Prompt

Take a few moments in your journal and answer:

1. What does *finishing strong* look like for me in this season of life?

2. What have I learned about God through my pain and healing?

3. What promise am I carrying into my next chapter?

Write freely. Let your heart speak. Then close your journal with a word of thanks: because your story is not ending here. It is only beginning again, with greater faith, deeper peace, and renewed, more profound.

HEALING PURPOSE WORKBOOK

A: Scriptures for Healing and Forgiveness

Write these scriptures in your journal. Circle the one that speaks to you most today.

- *"He heals the brokenhearted and binds up their wounds."* **(Psalm 147:3)**

- *"See, I am doing a new thing! Now it springs up; do you not perceive it?"* **(Isaiah 43:19)**

- *"For if you forgive other people when they sin against you, your heavenly Father will also forgive you."* **(Matthew 6:14)**

- *"Therefore, there is now no condemnation for those who are in Christ Jesus."* **(Romans 8:1)**

- *"If anyone is in Christ, he is a new creation; the old has gone, the new is here."* **(2 Corinthians 5:17)**

- *"I came that they may have life, and have it abundantly."* **(John 10:10)**

Reflection Space:

Notes

B: Daily Affirmations for Strength

Speak these aloud each morning. Then write your own personal affirmation.

1. I am whole and complete in Christ.

2. I release the past and walk in freedom.

3. I am worthy of love, joy, and peace.

4. God is restoring everything that was broken.

5. I choose forgiveness, and I choose life.

6. My future is filled with hope.

7. I am stronger today than I was yesterday.

My Personal Affirmation:

Notes

C: The A.R.E. Framework at a Glance

Acknowledge: Recognize and name the pain without shame.

Release: Let go of bitterness, regret, and fear into God's hands.

Empower: Step into your God-given identity and future with confidence.

Today I will...

- Acknowledge:

  ____

  ____

- Release:

  ____

  ____

- Empower:

  ____

  ____

D: Practical Healing Tools

- **Journaling:** Write down prayers, emotions, and reflections daily.

- **Vision Board:** Create a visual reminder of your new chapter.

- **Prayer Partner:** Walk with someone who can encourage and pray with you.

- **Self-Care Plan:** Choose habits that nourish your body, mind, and spirit.

Design My Self-Care Plan:

- Body:

  ____

  ____

- Mind:

  ____

  ____

- Spirit:

  ____

  ____

E: Reflection Questions for Small Groups or Personal Study

1. Which chapter of this book spoke most directly to your current season of life, and why?

2. What does forgiveness mean to you today?

3. What scripture from this book will you carry daily?

4. Where are you still holding on to old labels or pain?

5. How can you support someone else's healing while nurturing your own?

My Reflections:

Notes

F: Resources and Next Steps

- **Workbooks:** *Finding Peace in the Storm* (Companion Workbook)

- **Retreats:** *Healing the Heart Retreat* — visit www.debramwright.com

- **Coaching:** Personal and group coaching with Debra M. Wright at www.debramwright.com

- **Speaking Engagements:** For conferences, women's groups, or church events, contact debra@debramwright.com.

Your journey does not end here. Keep walking in faith, forgiveness, and freedom.

Media Attributions

- Beige Pink Illustrated Pet Journal Lined Note Page With Hearts and Pawprints

AFTERWORD

As you close these pages, I pray that you feel lighter, freer, and filled with hope for the future God is writing for you. Healing is not a straight line, but every step you take toward forgiveness is a step into freedom. My encouragement to you is this: do not stop here. Keep choosing life, keep choosing faith, and keep choosing to walk boldly in your God-given purpose.

Remember that the process of healing and forgiveness is an ongoing one. Some days, you will feel strong, and on other days, the old wounds may sting again. That does not mean you have failed. It means you are still on the journey, and God is still with you. Continue to lean on His promises, surround yourself with people who uplift you, and permit yourself to grow.

You are proof that brokenness is not the end of the story. With each new choice, you are stepping into the abundant life Jesus promised. May you rise daily with courage, walk in peace, and stand as a living testimony of God's unfailing grace.

Closing Blessing

May the Lord heal every place in you that still feels broken.

May His peace quiet the storms of your heart,
and may His joy rise within you like the morning sun.

May you walk each day with the confidence of one who is deeply loved,
forgiven, and chosen for a greater purpose.

May your steps be steady, your spirit be strong, and
 Your life is a light that shines hope into the world.

As you leave these pages, remember that your story is not over.
It is being written daily by the hand of a faithful God who turns ashes into beauty and sorrow into song.

Go forward in courage, in freedom, and in love.
You are not just standing, but you are rising.

RESOURCES FOR YOUR JOURNEY

To go deeper into healing and forgiveness, explore these additional resources created to support you:

- **Workbook:** *Finding Peace in the Storm* (Companion Journal & Study Guide)

- **Retreats:** *Healing the Heart Retreat* (visit https://www.debramwright.com for dates and details)

- **Coaching:** One-on-one and group coaching programs through **Debra M. Wright Coaching & Consulting**

- Join our Facebook Group: https://www.facebook.com/groups/ forgivenessafterdivorce

- **Speaking Engagements:** For events, workshops, and conferences, please get in touch with https://www.debramwright.com/book-me

ABOUT THE AUTHOR

Debra M. Wright is an Award-Winning Life Coach, Forgiveness Facilitator, Best-selling author, and inspirational speaker whose mission is to help women heal from trauma, divorce, and broken relationships. With compassion and clarity, she guides others through the journey of letting go of pain and embracing a life of freedom, peace, and renewed purpose.

At the heart of her work is her signature **A.R.E. framework: Acknowledge, Release, Empower is** a transformative process that equips women to face their past with honesty, release the burdens that hold them back, and step boldly into the identity and calling God designed for them.

Debra is the Founder and Executive Director of **Upward Springs Inc.,** a nonprofit organization serving immigrant families, marginalized women, and youth. **RMKI Publishing provides** a platform for stories of resilience, faith, and empowerment.

She hosts transformational retreats, leads empowerment cohorts, and writes books and plays that highlight the power of forgiveness and the transformative impact of faith in action.

When Debra is not writing, speaking, or coaching, she enjoys travelling, walking along the water, and cherishing time with her family, including her children and grandchildren, who are her constant inspiration.

Connect with Debra:

- Website: https://www.debramwright.com/
- Instagram: https://www.instagram.com/thereal_debramwright/
- Facebook: https://www.facebook.com/Debrawright21
- Email: shatteredbutstanding1@gmail.com

Media Attributions

- 7D5125EC-4C40-49E6-9F0A-57C83F686524

BOOKS BY AUTHOR

These books are on Amazon
Becoming Debra Wright: https://a.co/d/16s1eES

Pursued By Purpose: https://a.co/d/3mXRQ5A
Healing After Divorce: https://a.co/d/1lYYvGD

Media Attributions

- purse
- healing after
- becoming1